First Encyclopedia

REVISED EDITION
Editor Suneha Dutta
Assistant art editors Shreya Sadhan, Kartik Gera
Senior editor Shatarupa Chaudhuri
DTP designer Bimlesh Tiwary
Managing editors Alka Thakur Hazarika, Laura Gilbert
Managing art editors Romi Chakraborty, Diane Peyton Jones
CTS manager Balwant Singh
Publisher Sarah Larter
Senior producer, pre-production Ben Marcus
Producer Nicole Landau
Jacket editor Laura Gilbert
Jacket designer Diane Peyton Jones
Publishing director Sophie Mitchell
Publishing art director Stuart Jackman
Consultants John Woodward, Susan Kennedy,
Jack Challoner, Carole Scott

ORIGINAL EDITION
Authors Anita Ganeri, Chris Oxlade
Project editor Simon Holland
Senior art editor Tory Gordon-Harris
Editor Sue Malyan
Art editor Rebecca Johns
Managing editors Mary Ling, Sue Leonard
Managing art editors Rachael Foster, Cathy Chesson
Jacket designer Sophia Tampakopoulos MTT
Picture researcher Brenda Clynch
Production controller Jenny Jacoby
DTP designer Almudena Díaz

First American Edition, 2002
This American Edition, 2015
Published in the United States by DK Publishing, Inc.
345 Hudson Street, New York, NY 10014
A Penguin Random House Company

15 16 17 18 19 10 9 8 7 6 5 4 3 2 1
001–KJ006–Jun/2015

A catalog record for this title is available
from the Library of Congress.

ISBN 978-1-4654-3556-9

DK books are available at special discounts when purchased
in bulk for sales promotions, premiums, fund-raising, or
educational use. For details, contact: DK Publishing Special
Markets, 345 Hudson Street, New York, New York 10014 or
SpecialSales@dk.com.

Printed and bound in Hong Kong

A WORLD OF IDEAS:
SEE ALL THERE IS TO KNOW

Contents

World regions

People and society

History of people

Living world

This book will ask you lots of tricky questions...

Science and technology

Planet Earth

Space and the universe

Reference section

About this book

The pages of this book have special features that will show you how to get your hands on as much information as possible! Look for these:

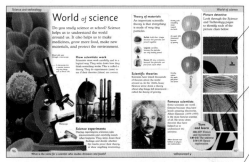

The Picture Detective quiz will get you searching through each chapter for the answers.

Turn and Learn will tell you which pages to turn to to look for more information on a subject.

Every page is color-coded to show you which chapter it is in.

hands on Activities show you how you can try things out for yourself.

World map

A world map, like the one below, shows what the world would look like if it were stretched out. People had to travel far and wide around the world before maps like this could be made.

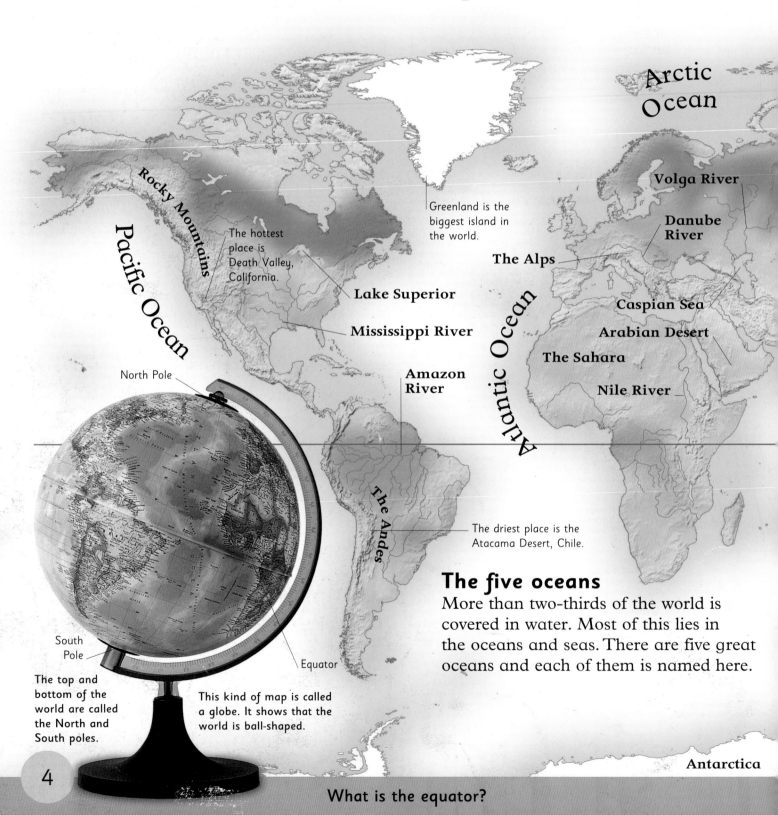

Arctic Ocean

Rocky Mountains

Pacific Ocean

Volga River

Danube River

The Alps

Greenland is the biggest island in the world.

The hottest place is Death Valley, California.

Lake Superior

Mississippi River

Caspian Sea

Arabian Desert

The Sahara

Atlantic Ocean

Amazon River

Nile River

North Pole

The Andes

The driest place is the Atacama Desert, Chile.

The five oceans

More than two-thirds of the world is covered in water. Most of this lies in the oceans and seas. There are five great oceans and each of them is named here.

South Pole

Equator

The top and bottom of the world are called the North and South poles.

This kind of map is called a globe. It shows that the world is ball-shaped.

Antarctica

4

Record-breakers

Here are some amazing physical features.

 The Sahara, in the northern part of Africa, is the world's biggest desert.

 Lake Superior, part of the "Great Lakes" in North America, is the largest freshwater lake.

 Mount Everest, in the Himalayan mountain range, Asia, is the highest mountain.

 The Nile River is the world's longest river. It snakes through Africa.

 The Pacific Ocean is the largest ocean. It covers about a third of the Earth.

Picture detective

Look through the World Regions pages and see if you can identify each of the picture clues below.

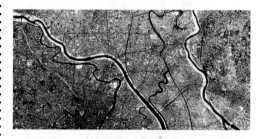

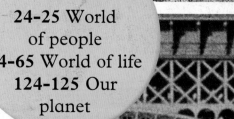

tains

Lake Baikal

Gobi Desert

alayas

nt
est

 Yangtze River

Physical features

This map shows the world's physical features. This means places like mountains, deserts, and lakes. Can you find the longest river on Earth?

The equator

Indian Ocean

Great Sandy Desert

Great Victoria Desert

Turn and learn

24-25 World of people
64-65 World of life
124-125 Our planet

The windiest place is Commonwealth Bay, Antarctica.

Southern Ocean

The coldest place is near Dome Argus, central Antarctica.

It is an imaginary line around the middle of the Earth.

Countries and continents

The world is divided into more than 190 countries in seven continents. Each country usually has its own leaders and makes it own laws.

North America is made up of Canada, the United States, and Mexico. The US has 50 states.

The world's seven continents

North America

South America

Ancient continents

Millions of years ago, the continents were joined together with a huge sea around them. Slowly, they split up and moved apart.

The continents 200 million years ago

Rivers, mountains, and seas make natural borders between countries.

The continents 135 million years ago

The continents 10 million years ago

Countries

On this map, you can see the different countries in the continent of South America. Some countries are tiny. Others, such as Brazil, are huge.

South America is the fourth-largest continent.

Caracas

Georgetown

Venezuela

Bogotá

Paramaribo

Cayenne

Colombia

Quito

Guyana

Equador

Surinam

Peru

French Guiana

São Paulo, in Brazil, is one of the world's largest cities. It has more than 11 million people.

Lima

Brazil

La Paz

Brasília

Bolivia

Sucre

São Paulo

Paraguay

Asunción

Chile

Uruguay

Santiago

Buenos Aires

Montevideo

Argentina

These are the Falkland Islands.

Capital cities

A country's most important city is called the capital. This is where the country's government meets and makes laws. Buenos Aires is the capital of Argentina.

Buenos Aires

Which country has the most neighbors?

The continents today

You can see the position of today's seven continents on the map below. Can you find the continent that contains your home country?

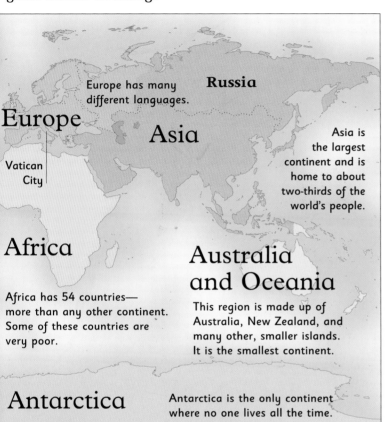

Europe

Europe has many different languages.

Russia

Asia

Vatican City

Asia is the largest continent and is home to about two-thirds of the world's people.

Africa

Africa has 54 countries—more than any other continent. Some of these countries are very poor.

Australia and Oceania

This region is made up of Australia, New Zealand, and many other, smaller islands. It is the smallest continent.

Antarctica

Antarctica is the only continent where no one lives all the time.

The biggest country

Russia is the biggest country in the world. It covers more than 6.8 million square miles (17 million square km) and stretches across both Europe and Asia.

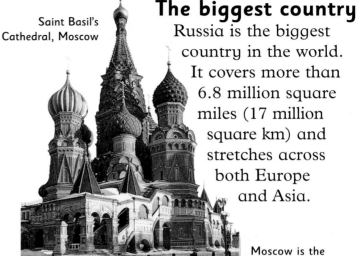

Saint Basil's Cathedral, Moscow

Moscow is the capital of Russia.

The smallest country

The Vatican City in Rome, Italy, is the smallest country. Only about 1,000 people live in the Vatican City.

Making maps

Maps used to be drawn by hand. Today, planes and satellites take pictures of the landscape. These are fed into computers, which turn them into maps.

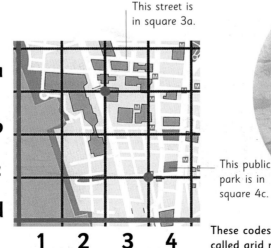

This street is in square 3a.

This public park is in square 4c.

These codes are called grid references.

Using a grid

Some maps have a grid plan, which helps you to find where a place is. On this map, each square has its own letter and number.

hands on

Maps of the countries and continents are grouped together in books called atlases. See if you can find an atlas and use it to find your home country.

China—it has 16 countries around it.

Seas and oceans

About two-thirds of the Earth's surface is covered in salty sea. This vast sea is made up of five oceans—the Pacific, Atlantic, Indian, Southern, and Arctic. These oceans all flow into each other.

Why the sea is salty

Seawater tastes salty because it has salt, and other minerals, dissolved in it. The salt mostly washes into the sea from the land. This is the same type of salt that you sprinkle on your food.

Many coral reef fish have colors that help them to blend in and hide from predators, or to look dangerous, which is a warning to predators.

Volcanoes and islands

Under the sea, there are mountains, valleys, plains, and volcanoes, just as there are on land. Some volcanoes are so tall that their tops poke out of the water and form islands.

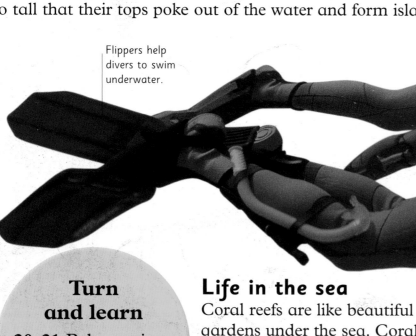

Flippers help divers to swim underwater.

Turn and learn

20-21 Polar regions
126-127 Volcanoes and earthquakes
134-135 Water

Life in the sea

Coral reefs are like beautiful gardens under the sea. Coral is made of the skeletons of millions of tiny sea animals. Thousands of sharks, fish, and other creatures live on coral reefs.

Which is the biggest coral reef in the world?

Oceans in motion

The water in the oceans is always moving. Great bands of water, called currents, flow like rivers in the sea and the wind blows the water into waves. Every day, the ocean tides rise and fall.

Frozen ocean

The Arctic Ocean is the world's smallest ocean. It is also the coldest. For most of the year, it is frozen over. This means that the North Pole is in the middle of a huge area of floating ice.

Special ships called ice-breakers can cut a path through the floating ice.

Blacktip reef shark

Coral

The Great Barrier Reef, off the northeastern coast of Australia.

Deserts

A long line of camels, called a caravan, crosses the Takla Makan Desert in China.

Deserts are the driest places on Earth. Sometimes no rain falls in the desert for years and years. By day, deserts may be baking hot, but at night they can be freezing cold.

Desert animals

Animals that live in the desert have special ways of staying cool and finding water. Camels have fat stored in their humps, so can go for days without food or water. This makes them very useful for desert travel.

Sand dunes can gradually creep forward and sometimes...

Sand is made from tiny fragments of rock.

This is a Saguaro cactus.

Desert plants

Some desert plants, such as this giant cactus, store water in their thick stems. Cacti are covered with sharp spines to stop hungry creatures from eating them. Cacti grow in American deserts.

Sandy deserts

Some deserts, such as the Namib Desert in Africa, are covered in vast seas of sand. The wind blows the sand into huge piles, called sand dunes. Some dunes can be 650 ft (200 m) high.

Which is the world's largest desert?

These desert mountains have been shaped by wind-blown sand.

These flat-topped rock formations are called buttes. These buttes, in Monument Valley in the US, have been named "Mitten Rocks."

Rocky deserts

These deserts are made of rocky plains covered in pebbles and gravel. The wind blows sand against the rocks, carving them into fantastic shapes.

Desert people

Some desert people are nomads. Nomads wander from place to place looking for food and water. They live in tents, which are easy to move.

.. bury whole villages under sand.

Water in the desert

In some places, water from deep underground seeps up to the surface. This is called an oasis. Here, trees and plants can grow, and people can find drinking water.

The Sahara in Africa.

Grasslands

Grasslands are dusty plains that are too dry for many plants to grow. There are grasslands in many parts of the world.

Some of the world's largest grasslands are shown on this map.

Grassland trees

Few trees grow in grasslands because the soil is too sandy and dry. Baobab trees survive by storing water in their huge trunks. The trunks shrink as the water is used up.

African grasslands

Many different animals live in grasslands, and a lot of them eat the grass that grows there. In an African grassland, large herds of zebras roam the plains, together with impalas, wildebeest, elephants, and giraffes.

Turn and learn

68-69 Trees and forests
74-75 Mammals
136-137 Weather

Grassland animals travel long distances to drink at a waterhole.

How many different types of grass are there?

Grasslands

The prairies

In North America, grasslands are called prairies. Large parts of the prairies have been turned into fields where farmers grow wheat and other crops.

Huge areas of Pampas are covered in spiked pampas grass.

The Pampas

The southern grasslands of South America are called Pampas. They are home to some unusual animals, such as giant anteaters, vizcachas (burrowing rodents), and rheas (flightless birds).

Wheat being harvested on an American prairie field

Animal scavengers

Some grassland animals, such as vultures, are scavengers. They soar above the ground looking for dead animals. Then they swoop down to feed on the scraps.

A white-backed vulture is on the lookout for food.

Tough plants, such as grasses and thorny trees, can grow in the grasslands.

Impalas are hunted by animals such as cheetahs and jackals.

Rain forests

Rain forests are hot, steamy jungles that grow near the equator. They are home to more than half of all the types of plant and animal on Earth.

Rain forests are hot and steamy because they grow mainly in the warm areas near the equator, called the tropics.

North America

Europe

Asia

Africa

Equator

Amazon Rain Forest

South America

Australia and Oceania

The world's biggest tropical rain forests are shown in green on this map.

Rain forests cover a small part of Earth but contain thousands of plants and animals.

Forest layers

Rain forest trees grow in layers. Each layer has its own plants, insects, birds, and animals.

The emergent layer has the tallest trees. Their tops tower above the ground.

The canopy is like a thick, green umbrella. Most animals live here.

The understory has shorter trees, covered in creepers and vines.

The forest floor is gloomy, dark, and covered in dead leaves, fungi, and ferns.

Animals

Every part of the rain forest is alive with animals, from spectacular butterflies to parrots, frogs, snakes, jaguars, and millions of creepy-crawlies.

Which are the most dangerous ants of all?

Rain forest riches
Food, wood, medicines, and other useful products come from rain forest plants. Even chocolate comes from the beans of a rain forest tree.

Doctors use the rosy periwinkle plant to treat leukemia, a blood disease.

Biggest rain forest
The world's biggest rain forest grows along the banks of the Amazon River in South America. The forest is about the same size as Australia.

Hot and wet
In the rain forest, the weather is hot and wet all year round. This orangutan is sheltering from the pouring rain under an umbrella of leaves.

Some orchids dangle their roots in the air to soak up water.

Plants
The steamy rain forest heat is ideal for many plants to bloom. Some plants, such as these beautiful orchids, grow high up on the branches of the canopy trees.

Turn and learn
66-67 Plant life
68-69 Trees and forests
138-139 Climate and seasons

15

Army ants. They attack and kill animals.

Rivers and lakes

Many rivers start as a stream or spring, high up on a mountainside. As the water flows downhill, other streams flow into it to make a river.

Waterfalls

When a river flows over bands of soft and hard rock, it wears the soft rock away. This leaves a step of hard rock, which the river plunges over. This makes a waterfall.

Stages of a river

At first, a river flows very fast. It slows down as it reaches flat land, where it drops sand and mud that it has carried from the hills. Finally, the river flows into the ocean.

A steamboat on the Mississippi River in the US

River transportation

For thousands of years, people have used rivers to carry people, animals, and goods. Barges, steamboats, and canoes are different types of river transportation.

What is the world's longest river?

River life

Many amazing animals are suited to life in or near the world's rivers.

Piranhas are ferocious fish with razor-sharp teeth for snapping up their prey.

Otters are rare animals with sleek, streamlined bodies for swimming.

Crocodiles hide in the water, then leap out to grab their prey.

Water boatmen are insects that use their legs to row across the water.

Salty lakes

Some lakes are filled with salty water. The Dead Sea, between Israel and Jordan, is so salty that you can float in it while reading a newspaper!

This lake is called the Dead Sea because no fish can live there.

Turn and learn

Many lakes form high up in the mountains, where ice has carved out a hollow.

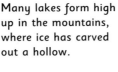

Lakes

A lake is a large stretch of water surrounded by land. It is made when rain or river water fills a large hollow or dip in the ground.

Largest lakes

The world's biggest freshwater lake is Lake Superior in the US and Canada. It is part of a group of five huge lakes called the Great Lakes.

Curved beaks help to strain lake water for food.

Flamingos get their pink color from the food they eat.

Lesser flamingos

Lake life

Lakes are home to hundreds of plants and animals. Huge flocks of brightly colored flamingos build their nests on the shores of some lakes in Africa.

The Nile River in Africa.

Mountains

When two huge chunks of the Earth's rocky crust crash or push into each other, a mighty mountain is made.

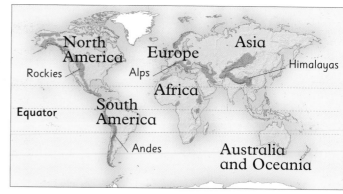

Some of the world's biggest mountain ranges are shown in brown on this map

The high life

High up on a mountainside, it is cold and windy. The air is thin and hard to breathe. Despite this, many people live in the mountains. The people in this picture come from Tibet in Asia.

Mount Everest

Most of the world's highest mountain peaks are in Asia. Everest, in the Himalayas, is the highest mountain on Earth. It is 29,035 ft (8,850 m) tall.

Mount Everest

The Himalayas are the world's highest mountain range.

What does the name "Himalaya" mean?

Mountain danger

Sometimes huge amounts of ice and snow break loose and crash down a mountainside. This is called an avalanche. The snow can bury people, and even whole villages, in its path.

Mountain animals

Despite the extreme weather, many animals live in the mountains.

Snow leopards from the Himalayas have thick fur coats to keep them warm.

Spectacled bears from the Andes eat leaves, fruit, eggs, and small mammals.

Mountain gorillas from Africa have been hunted and are very rare.

Golden eagles soar high above the mountain peaks of Europe.

Mountain lions are fast, clever hunters from North and South America.

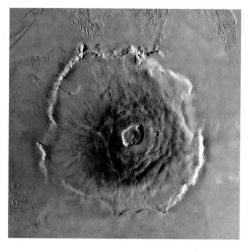

Mountains on Mars

Did you know that there are mountains on other planets? This is Olympus Mons on Mars. It is a gigantic volcano, three times higher than Mount Everest. The crater on top is the size of two large cities.

This strong rope would hold the climber if he fell.

The climber's boots help him to grip the rock.

Mountain sports

Many people enjoy walking, climbing, and skiing in the mountains. Some mountain sports can be dangerous, so people use special safety equipment.

Home of the snows.

Polar regions

The poles are at the top and bottom of the Earth. They are the coldest places on the planet, with ice as far as the eye can see.

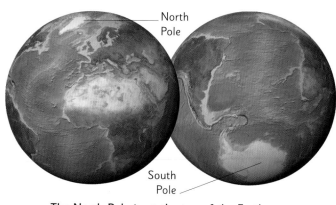

North Pole

South Pole

The North Pole is at the top of the Earth. The South Pole is at the bottom.

The Arctic

The Arctic is the region around the North Pole. The pole lies in the middle of the icy Arctic Ocean, which freezes over for most of the year.

Polar bears can travel long distances using huge pieces of ice as rafts.

Arctic people

People have lived in the Arctic for thousands of years. They are experts at surviving in the cold. These Inuit children are dressed in their warm, winter clothes.

Life on the tundra

The tundra is a vast, icy area around the Arctic. It is frozen in winter but thaws out in summer. Caribou graze on the tundra plants.

Inuit people sometimes use skidoos (sleds with motors) to race across the icy ground.

In addition to Antarctica, where do penguins live?

Antarctica

The region around the South Pole is called Antarctica. Antarctica is a large piece of land covered in a thick sheet of ice. Antarctica is one of the seven continents. It is bigger than Europe.

Halley Station, Antarctica

Antarctic mountains

Antarctic science

Despite the cold conditions, thousands of scientists work in Antarctica. They spend their time studying the ice, the wildlife, and the weather. They live at research stations like this one.

Antarctic wildlife

Some amazing animals live in Antarctica. Emperor penguins have thick, waterproof and windproof feathers, with a layer of fat underneath. This keeps them warm and dry in the freezing temperatures.

Emperor penguin chicks are born in the middle of winter.

Turn and learn

38-39 Clothes and fashion
124-125 Our planet
134-135 Water

The coasts of South America, Africa, Australia, New Zealand, and the Galápagos Islands

Great cities

Millions of people live and work in the world's cities. People also visit cities to go shopping and to see the sights.

The Empire State Building is New York's most famous skyscraper.

Rio de Janeiro

Rio is the second-biggest city in Brazil. It is surrounded by steep hills and beautiful beaches. There are stylish apartment blocks, but many poor people live in Rio's "shanty towns" (slums).

Paris

The beautiful city of Paris is the capital of France. The city's most famous landmark is the Eiffel Tower. Paris has many fine clothing stores, restaurants, and street cafés.

The Tower of London

You can see the whole of Paris from any of the Eiffel Tower's three viewing floors.

London

London is the capital city of England and the United Kingdom. It is one of the world's most important business centers. London has many famous palaces, churches, and bridges.

New York

New York is the largest city in the US. This city is famous for its skyscrapers and yellow taxis. People from all over the world live in New York.

What city is the capital of Russia?

Capital cities

A country's capital is the city where its government meets. Here are some record-breaking capital cities.

Tokyo, in Japan, is the biggest capital, with more than 27 million people.

Damascus, in Syria, is the oldest capital. People have lived there for 2,500 years.

Lhasa, in Tibet, is the world's highest capital at 12,087 ft (3,684 m).

Reykjavik, in Iceland, is the world's most northerly capital city.

Wellington, in New Zealand, is the world's most southerly capital.

Shanghai

Shanghai is one of the biggest cities in China. The old part of the city has narrow, crowded streets. Shanghai is one of the world's largest ports and has factories that make steel and ships.

Cairo

Cairo is the capital of Egypt. Its old streets are full of markets called bazaars. The ancient pyramids stand in the desert on the edge of the modern city.

The pyramids were built about 4,500 years ago by ancient Egyptians.

Sydney harbor

Sydney

Sydney is Australia's largest and oldest city. The Sydney Opera House looks over the city's harbor, where there is a huge port. The Olympic Games were held in Sydney in 2000.

Turn and learn
4-5 World map
48-49 Ancient Egypt
62-63 20th century
116-117 Engineering

Moscow.

World of people

More than seven billion people live in the world. These people have different customs, languages, beliefs, and lifestyles.

This girl is dressed up for May Day—a festival that is celebrated in some parts of Europe.

Language and people

One in every five people in the world lives in China. The most widely spoken language is Mandarin Chinese, which has almost one billion speakers.

Culture

People enjoy many different kinds of art and culture.

 Writing is used to record information, news, views, stories, and history.

 Theater entertains audiences with acting, dance, and costume.

 Painting is a way of expressing feelings and ideas through pictures.

 Fashion is different all over the world, and it is changing all the time.

 Music styles can be classical or popular, traditional or modern.

May Day marks the first day of spring, after the long, cold months of winter.

24

At work

All over the world, people work to earn a living. What job would you like to do? You could be an astronaut or a teacher, a farmer or a computer programmer.

At play

Having time for leisure and play is very important. Some people like watching or playing sports. Like these children, you might enjoy playing games with friends.

Celebrations

Important times in people's lives are celebrated with special feasts and festivals. These are times for people to enjoy themselves and to share their religious and cultural beliefs.

At some festivals in India, people exchange gifts of sweets, like these.

Picture detective

Look through the People and Society pages and see if you can identify the picture clues below.

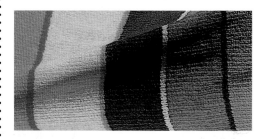

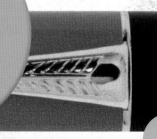

Turn and learn

4-5 World map
44-45 World of history
88-89 Human body

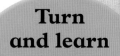

Spanish.

Religious lands

Many people follow a religion. A religion is a set of beliefs and a way of worship. The main religions today are Hinduism, Judaism, Buddhism, Christianity, Islam, and Sikhism.

Hinduism

Hinduism began in India about 4,000 years ago. Hindus believe in a supreme being called Brahman. They worship many gods and goddesses, who represent different parts of Brahman.

Hindus bathing in the holy Ganges River in India

Rosary

The Church of the Holy Sepulcher, in Jerusalem

Sacred symbols

Each of these symbols has a special meaning.

 In **Hinduism**, the "Aum" symbol represents the first sound of creation.

 In **Judaism**, the Star of David reminds Jews of a great Jewish king.

 In **Buddhism**, the spokes of the wheel represent the eight points of the Buddha's teaching.

 In **Christianity**, the cross reminds Christians of Jesus' death on a cross.

 In **Islam**, the star and crescent moon appear on many Islamic flags.

 In **Sikhism**, the khanda symbol reminds Sikhs of God and of God's power.

Christianity

Christians follow the teachings of a man named Jesus Christ who lived about 2,000 years ago. They believe that Jesus was the son of God, who died to save them from sin.

What is the Christian holy book called?

This building is a Buddhist monastery in Thailand.

Islam

People who follow Islam are called Muslims. They believe in Allah (God), who guides them through their lives. The holy book of Islam is called the Qur'an (Koran). It contains the word of God as revealed to the Prophet Mohammed.

Mecca (Makkah) is a holy city for Muslims.

Western Wall

The Western Wall (Wailing Wall), in Jerusalem, is a holy place for Jews.

Buddhism

Buddhists follow the teachings of the Buddha. He was an Indian prince who lived about 2,500 years ago. He showed people how to live good, happy lives, full of peace.

Statues of the Buddha often show him meditating (focusing the mind).

Menorah (Jewish candlestick)

Judaism

Judaism is the religion of the Jews. Their holy book is called the Torah. It tells the story of the Jewish people and their special relationship with God.

Turn and learn

32-33 Art and architecture
48-49 Ancient Egypt
54-55 The Vikings

The Golden Temple in Amritsar, India, is the holiest of all Sikh shrines.

Sikhism

The Sikh religion was started by a teacher named Guru Nanak. Sikhs worship in a building called a gurdwara. Their holy book is the Guru Granth Sahib.

The Bible.

Religious life

In their religious lives, people honor their God or gods. They may come together for worship and celebrate special events with feasts and festivals.

Statue of the Buddha

Islam
Muslims (followers of Islam) must pray five times a day: at dawn, noon, midafternoon, sunset, and nighttime. Muslims follow a set of special prayer positions.

Buddhism
Buddhists do not worship a god, but honor the life and teachings of the Buddha. In the temple, they offer flowers, candles, and incense to the Buddha to show their respect.

In some Buddhist countries, boys spend time as monks.

What is a mosque?

In a synagogue, Jews listen to readings from the Torah, their holy book.

Torah scroll

Silver pointer

Judaism

Jewish people meet to worship and pray in a special building called a synagogue. A man or woman called a rabbi leads the worship.

Turban

Small sword

Steel bangle

This is Ganesha, the elephant-headed god.

Hinduism

Hindus worship the gods and goddesses in their homes and in mandirs (temples). The god Ganesha is said to bring good luck and success.

Sikhism

Many Sikh men wear five things to show their faith. These are uncut hair (often kept neatly in a turban), a wooden comb, a small sword, a steel bangle, and white underpants.

Christianity

Christmas is a joyful festival when Christians remember how Jesus was born. There are services in church, and people celebrate by exchanging cards and gifts.

Jesus was born in a stable in Bethlehem. Three kings brought gifts for him.

Joseph

These children are acting out the story of the first Christmas.

Three kings

Jesus

Mary

A building where Muslims worship Allah (God).

Writing and printing

People began to write things down about 5,500 years ago. Before this, they told stories and passed news on by word of mouth. Today, writing is all around you.

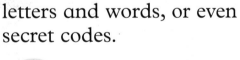
The alphabet

Fountain pens are filled with ink.

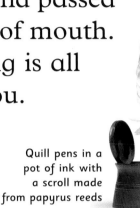
Quill pens in a pot of ink with a scroll made from papyrus reeds

Paper and pens
The paper you use today comes from trees. Long ago, people made paper from reeds or animal skins. The first pens were pieces of reeds dipped in soot or ink.

Signs and symbols
Sometimes, signs and symbols are used to write letters and words, or even secret codes.

Pictograms are pictures used for writing. This old, Chinese word means "to sell."

Hieroglyphs were used by the ancient Egyptians. This one stands for "chick."

Runes were Viking symbols that were carved on stone or wood. This is the "M" sound.

Music symbols like these are used to write down musical sounds (notes).

Morse code changes the alphabet into dot and dash signals for sending messages.

Writing machines
The first typewriters were invented about 200 years ago. They made writing much quicker. Today, modern word processors, like this laptop computer, are used instead.

Early typewriter   Laptop computer

How long did it take to create this book?

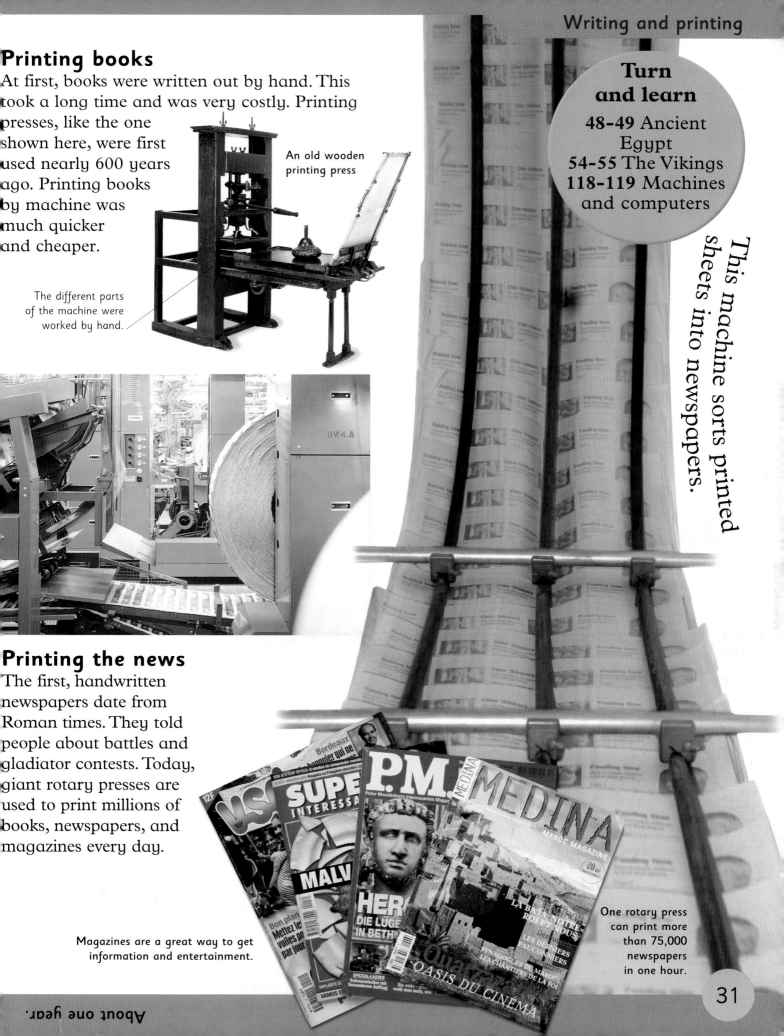

Printing books

At first, books were written out by hand. This took a long time and was very costly. Printing presses, like the one shown here, were first used nearly 600 years ago. Printing books by machine was much quicker and cheaper.

An old wooden printing press

The different parts of the machine were worked by hand.

Turn and learn

48-49 Ancient Egypt
54-55 The Vikings
118-119 Machines and computers

This machine sorts printed sheets into newspapers.

Printing the news

The first, handwritten newspapers date from Roman times. They told people about battles and gladiator contests. Today, giant rotary presses are used to print millions of books, newspapers, and magazines every day.

Magazines are a great way to get information and entertainment.

One rotary press can print more than 75,000 newspapers in one hour.

About one year.

Art and architecture

Since ancient times, artists have painted pictures and used stone and wood to make sculptures. Architects plan the world's buildings.

Cave painting
Prehistoric artists painted pictures of figures and animals on cave walls. This cave painting is from Africa.

Church art
The Italian artist Michelangelo painted scenes from the Bible on the ceiling and walls of the Sistine Chapel in Rome, Italy.

Modern sculpture
Modern British artist Henry Moore used bold shapes to create this interesting—and "touchable"—giant stone sculpture.

Skyscraper

Singapore skyline

Which is the world's tallest building?

Architecture

Every building you see has been planned by an architect. Styles of architecture have changed over thousands of years. Buildings are designed for living, working, worship, or simply for fun.

Castles were built to defend people from attack. This castle is in Spain.

Making art

People use different types of art to capture a scene or express their ideas. Here are a few of them.

Drawing a quick "sketch" in pencil is a way for artists to plan a color painting.

Painting can be done on paper using watercolors, or on canvas with oil paints.

Sculpting is the skill of making works of art out of stone, wood, metal, or clay.

Photography uses a film or digital camera to make images of people and places.

Graphic design combines words and images on a computer in colorful ways.

The Taj Mahal

The beautiful Taj Mahal in India was built by Emperor Shah Jahan as a tomb for his wife, Mumtaz Mahal. It is made from white marble, set with colored stones.

Modern skyscrapers make up the Singapore skyline.

An opera house

The Opera House in Sydney, Australia, is a modern building. Its winglike roof makes it easy to identify. It was designed to look like the sails of boats in the nearby harbor.

Turn and learn

22-23 Great cities
50-51 Ancient Greece
116-117 Engineering

The Burj Khalifa in Dubai. It is 2,717 ft (828 m) tall.

Music

What is your favorite song or tune? Do you like classical, jazz, folk, rock, or pop music? If you play a musical instrument, you can make music of your own.

Conductor

An orchestra

Some musicians perform together in a group called an orchestra. There are about 90 musicians in a symphony orchestra. The conductor keeps them in time. Orchestras usually play classical music.

Drums and cymbals are percussion instruments.

Cymbal

Drum

Musical instruments

In an orchestra, there are four kinds of instrument—brass, woodwind, percussion, and strings. Each instrument makes its own individual sound. The different sounds blend together.

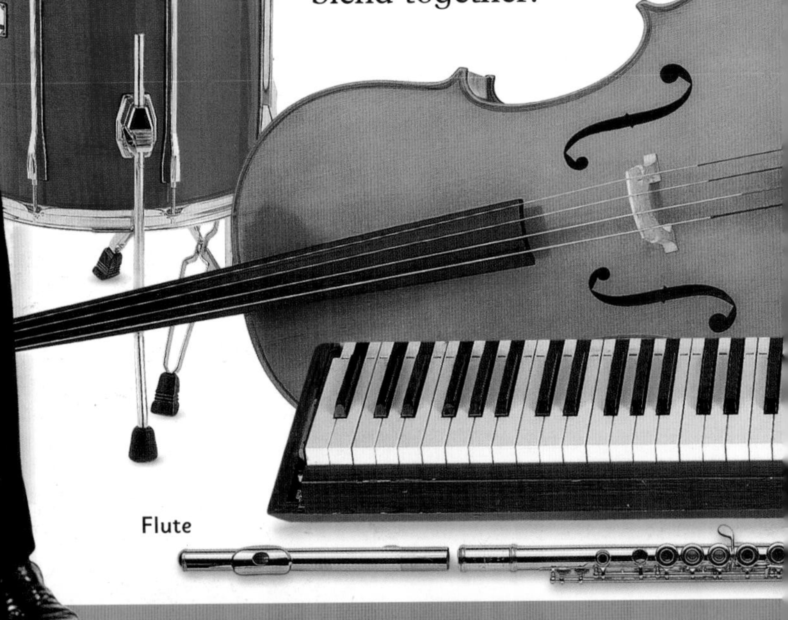

Flute

What kind of instrument is a xylophone?

Recording music

In a recording studio, each voice or instrument can be recorded on its own. These are called tracks. Engineers mix the tracks together.

Mixing desk

The knobs on the mixing desk control the volume and tone of each track.

Types of music

Many different kinds of music are played all over the world.

Early music was probably played on instruments made from animal bones.

Opera is a play set to music in which the performers sing their lines.

Jazz musicians make up some or all of the music as they play it.

Rock music, or rock and roll, has punchy lyrics (words) and a strong beat.

Pop is short for popular music. It has catchy tunes and is good for dancing.

Madonna is one of the most successful pop singers of all time.

Madonna

Vinyl record

CDs

Minidisc   Mp3 Player

You can listen to music on records, CDs, and Mp3 players, as well as handheld devices and computers.

Many rock and pop musicians play music on electric guitars.

Concerts

Watching your favourite pop or rock star perform live on stage can be thrilling. Many people work behind the scenes to make the shows run smoothly.

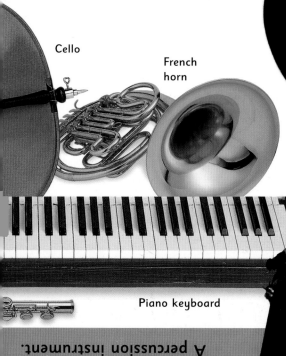

Cello

French horn

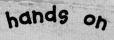

Piano keyboard

hands on

Would you like to be a rock star? Try writing your own song. Start by writing a poem, then make up a tune to go with it.

Theater and dance

Theater began thousands of years ago in ancient Greece. Actors and dancers put on shows to entertain and inform people.

Actors and acting

Putting on a play is a long task. First, the playwright writes the play. Then actors bring the story and the characters in the play to life. They also have to remember their lines!

Actors use their bodies, as well as the words, to create a character and perform the scenes.

These actors are playing two characters named Romeo and Juliet.

Costumes help to show when and where the play's action is happening.

Musical theater

Going to the theater to see a musical is a special treat. Musicals are an exciting mixture of acting, dancing, and song. This is a scene from the musical *Oliver!*

Who wrote the play *Romeo and Juliet*?

Japanese theater

These actors are performing an ancient type of Japanese play called Kabuki. They wear beautiful costumes and mix acting, singing, dancing, and music to put on a dazzling show.

Indian dance

Dancing is a way of telling a story or showing a feeling using movement and music. This type of dancing, from India, is made up of special movements and expressions.

Forms of dance

There are many different types and styles of dance from all over the world.

Tap dancers wear metal-capped shoes to make "tap" sounds.

Ballet is a graceful type of dance set to music that tells a tale.

Country and **folk** dances from around the world are lively and fun.

Flamenco is a dramatic Spanish dance set to the sound of clicking castanets.

Jazz dance uses the rhythm and beat of jazz music to create an exciting dance.

Puppet shows

Puppet shows are a very old type of theater. These glove puppets are simple to work. A hand inside makes the puppet move. One finger works the puppet's head, while two other fingers work the arms.

Punch and Judy are famous puppets from Britain.

Punch

Judy

Turn and learn

34-35 Music
50-51 Ancient Greece
120-121 Television and media

William Shakespeare.

Clothes and fashion

What are you wearing today? A T-shirt? Pants? Sneakers? Clothes can make you look good. They may also have a special job to do.

Types of fabric

Clothes are made from a variety of materials.

Cotton is made of fibers from the cotton plant. The fabric is usually woven.

Silk is a thin, soft fabric made from threads spun by silkworms.

Leather is made from the skins of animals, such as cows.

Wool is made from the hair of sheep. It is often knitted to make clothes.

Nylon and other **artificial fabrics** are made from chemicals.

This Vietnamese boy is wearing casual clothes.

This Indian girl is wearing a sari.

A raincoat, rain boots, and umbrella are useful when it rains.

This French girl wears a top and skirt for school.

What do you wear?

What you wear depends on where you live and what you are doing. People wear different clothes for keeping warm, staying cool, for playing sports, and for going to school.

38

What is a beret ("berr-eh")?

Fashion shows

Some people design clothes to look stylish or unusual. They are called fashion designers. They put on fashion shows where models show off their clothes.

Clothes for the cold

In cold climates, clothes were traditionally made from animal fur and skins. Today, synthetic (artificial) fabrics are often used instead.

This firefighter's uniform protects against heat and flames. Do you wear a uniform at school?

Uniforms

Some people have to wear special clothes for work. These are called uniforms. This firefighter's uniform protects against heat and flames. Do you wear a uniform at school?

This Masai girl from Tanzania is wearing her colorful national dress.

Children from the Arctic need thick, fur-lined clothes for warmth.

This outfit is the national dress of a hill tribe from Vietnam.

This girl is wearing a kimono, the national dress of Japan.

National dress

A country's traditional clothes are called its national dress. In many countries, people only wear their national dress for festivals or other special occasions.

Sports and leisure

What do you do in your spare time? Do you enjoy a favorite sport? Or do you have fun with toys or play computer games?

Soccer is the most popular sport in the world.

Spectator sports

A spectator sport is a sport that people like to watch. Soccer, basketball, football, baseball, and golf are all spectator sports.

Snowboarders wear warm, baggy clothes.

Snowboarders do amazing spins and jumps.

Plastic clips attach the boots to the snowboard.

Team sports

All of these spectator sports are played by two teams of players.

In **baseball**, teams score runs by batting. Fielders wear catching gloves.

In **basketball**, points are scored by throwing the ball into a raised hoop (basket).

In **soccer**, each team tries to kick or head the ball into the other team's net.

In **ice hockey**, teams score goals by hitting a puck with flat sticks.

In **rugby**, teams score "tries" by putting the oval ball over the opposing line.

Outdoor sports

Snowboarding, rock climbing, canoeing, skiing, and sailing are outdoor sports. You need special equipment and clothes to do outdoor sports safely.

Which games are played with cues on a table?

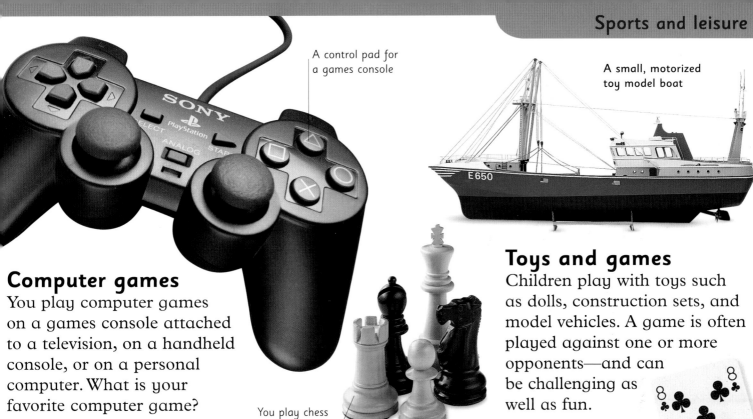

A control pad for a games console

A small, motorized toy model boat

E 650

Computer games

You play computer games on a games console attached to a television, on a handheld console, or on a personal computer. What is your favorite computer game?

You play chess with pieces on a board.

Toys and games

Children play with toys such as dolls, construction sets, and model vehicles. A game is often played against one or more opponents—and can be challenging as well as fun.

Playing cards

Doll

Individual sports

In these, people play on their own against one or more opponents.

In **tennis**, players hit a ball with rackets. They must keep the ball in the court.

While **swimming**, swimmers race each other up and down a pool.

In **golf**, players hit a ball around a course, using as few shots as they can.

While **running**, runners race against each other on a track or on roads.

In **table tennis**, players hit a ball with small bats. The game is played on a table.

Going to the movies

When new films are made, they are first shown on large screens at movie theaters. Today, many movies are made using animation and special effects.

Working people

What do you want to be when you grow up? All over the world, people do different kinds of work to earn the money to buy their food, clothes, and homes.

Astronauts

Astronauts are people who fly spacecraft and work in space. They conduct experiments in orbiting laboratories called space stations, and often spend months in space.

Market sellers

There are markets selling food and other goods in almost every town and city. This man is selling fruits and vegetables from his market stall in Cairo, Egypt.

What do you call someone who writes books to earn a living?

This vet is giving a dog a health check.

The farmer's plow is being pulled by an ox.

Vets

If your pet is sick, you take it to the vet. Vets look after sick and injured animals. Some vets treat small animals, such as cats and dogs. Others work with farm or zoo animals.

Farmers

All over the world, farmers grow crops and raise animals. They grow food for themselves and to sell at market. This farmer is plowing his rice field in Thailand.

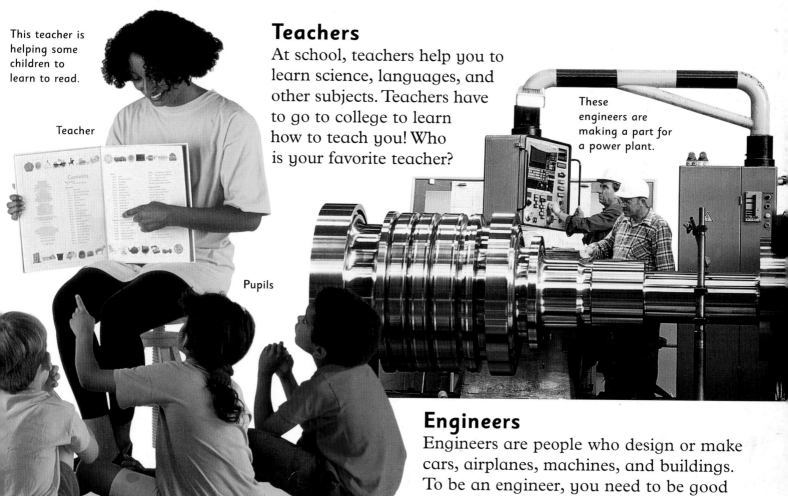

This teacher is helping some children to learn to read.

Teacher

Pupils

Teachers

At school, teachers help you to learn science, languages, and other subjects. Teachers have to go to college to learn how to teach you! Who is your favorite teacher?

These engineers are making a part for a power plant.

Engineers

Engineers are people who design or make cars, airplanes, machines, and buildings. To be an engineer, you need to be good at science and mathematics.

An author.

43

World of history

History tells us the story of how people lived in the past. From the things they left behind, we can find out about their homes, food, clothes, work, and beliefs.

Solid gold

Decorative blue stones called lapis lazuli

The mummy mask of the Egyptian king Tutankhamun

Early people
About 10,000 years ago, groups of people began to settle down in certain places. They started to farm the land and to raise animals for food.

Powerful kings
Many great civilizations were ruled by powerful kings. In ancient Egypt, the kings were called pharaohs. They were so important that people worshiped them as gods.

Early farmers cut down the ripe wheat stalks with a sickle made from a sharp flint stone set in a wooden handle.

People learned how to grow crops for food.

Spanish galleon

44

Greeks and Romans

About 2,500 years ago, ancient Greek culture flourished. Then, around 27 BCE, the Romans grew in strength and ruled over a great empire from Rome in Italy.

The ancient Acropolis in Athens, Greece

Explorers

For centuries, people have traveled far and wide across the world. They went in search of new lands, goods to trade, and adventures.

Now, people are exploring space.

The first Space Shuttle flight was made in 1981 with a Shuttle called *Columbia*.

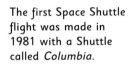

These coins were made by European explorers using the gold they discovered on their travels.

20th century

The 20th century saw many new inventions and discoveries being made. People flew in space for the first time, and even walked on the Moon.

Picture detective

Look through the History of People pages and see if you can identify the picture clues below.

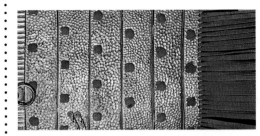

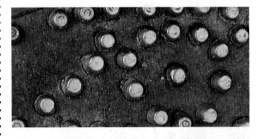

Turn and learn

30-31 Writing and printing
60-61 Explorers
152-153 Space travel

Homo habilis skull

Neanderthal skull

Modern human skull

From apes to human beings

Our oldest ancestors looked like apes. Slowly, they became more humanlike and began to walk upright on two legs.

Early people

The first human ancestors lived about four million years ago. We do not know exactly what they looked like, but we do know how they lived.

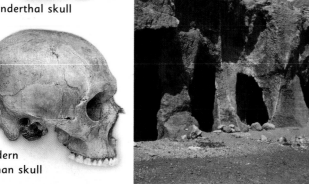

Cave shelters

Early people used caves like these as shelters. Inside, the caves were safe and warm. Sometimes, people painted the walls with pictures of the animals they hunted.

A flint hand ax from Egypt

The first farmers

About 10,000 years ago, people learned how to grow food from the ground. They were the first farmers. They also made pots to store grains, which they ground in stone grinders.

Fire

Flint blade

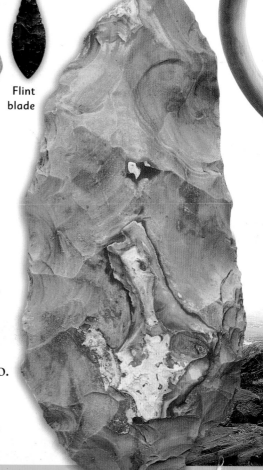

Tools and fire

We take fire and tools for granted, but early people had to learn how to make and use them. The first tools were stone choppers and knives, made about 2.6 million years ago.

This woman is grinding grain between two stones to make flour for bread.

How did early people start fires?

The first cities

When people started growing their food, they were able to settle in one place. They began to build houses, villages, and cities. One of the first cities was Jericho in Jordan.

Hunters and gatherers

Early people hunted woolly mammoths, cave bears, caribou, and other animals for food. They also collected fruit, nuts, and roots, and caught fish.

Early achievements

Here are some of the everyday things that early people used.

Dogs, one of the first animals to be **domesticated**, were used for hunting about 14,000 years ago.

The first **metal tools** were made from copper about 10,000 years ago.

The earliest **clay pots**, used for cooking, were made in Japan about 10,000 years ago.

Turn and learn

22-23 Great cities
128-129 Rocks and fossils

Mammoth hunting was dangerous work!

The meat from a mammoth was enough to feed a family for a whole year.

Hunters used wooden spears.

By rubbing two sticks or striking two stones together.

Ancient Egypt

The ancient Egyptians lived by the banks of the Nile River about 3,500 years ago. Their powerful rulers were called pharaohs.

Beautifully decorated mummy

The pyramids
The ancient Egyptians believed in life after death. The pharaohs built magnificent tombs, called pyramids, for themselves.

Mummy of a cat

Building skills
Egyptian builders did not have modern tools and machines to help them. The workers carried huge stone blocks into place, or sent them on barges along the river.

These men are carrying stone blocks for building, as the ancient Egyptians did.

Mummification
When an important person died, the body was "mummified." Some of the inside parts were removed. Then the body was treated with chemicals and wrapped in bandages.

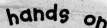

hands on

Try writing out a message using only Egyptian hieroglyphics. You can also make up your own set of hieroglyphic symbols.

48

Why did the Egyptians mummify their dead?

The Nile floods

Each year, the Nile River flooded and spread rich, black soil on its banks. Farmers grew crops in the soil and used the river water to water their fields.

The Nile River in Egypt

A funeral barge

Nile barges were used for transportation.

Hieroglyphics

The Egyptians used picture writing called hieroglyphics. Symbols, such as those below, stood for letters and sounds.

Hieroglyphs

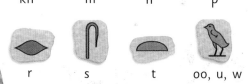

ah	b	c, k	d
ee, y	f	g	h
kh	m	n	p
r	s	t	oo, u, w

Hieroglyphic sound chart

The Sphinx

A huge stone statue, called the Sphinx, guards the pyramids at Giza. It has the body of a lion and a human head, which was modeled on the pharaoh's own features.

The Sphinx is carved out of one massive stone.

The great Sphinx guards the pyramid of Pharaoh Khafra.

To keep the body whole for the next life.

Ancient Greece

About 2,500 years ago, Greece was made up of powerful city-states, such as Athens and Sparta, that fought wars against each other.

Greek buildings
The ancient Greeks built beautiful temples where they worshiped their gods. This temple in Athens was built to honor the goddess Athena.

Greek theater
Going to the theater was very popular in ancient Greece. The Greeks wrote many plays, both tragedies and comedies. People watched their favorite plays in large outdoor theaters, like the one above.

Turn and learn

Where were the first Olympic Games held?

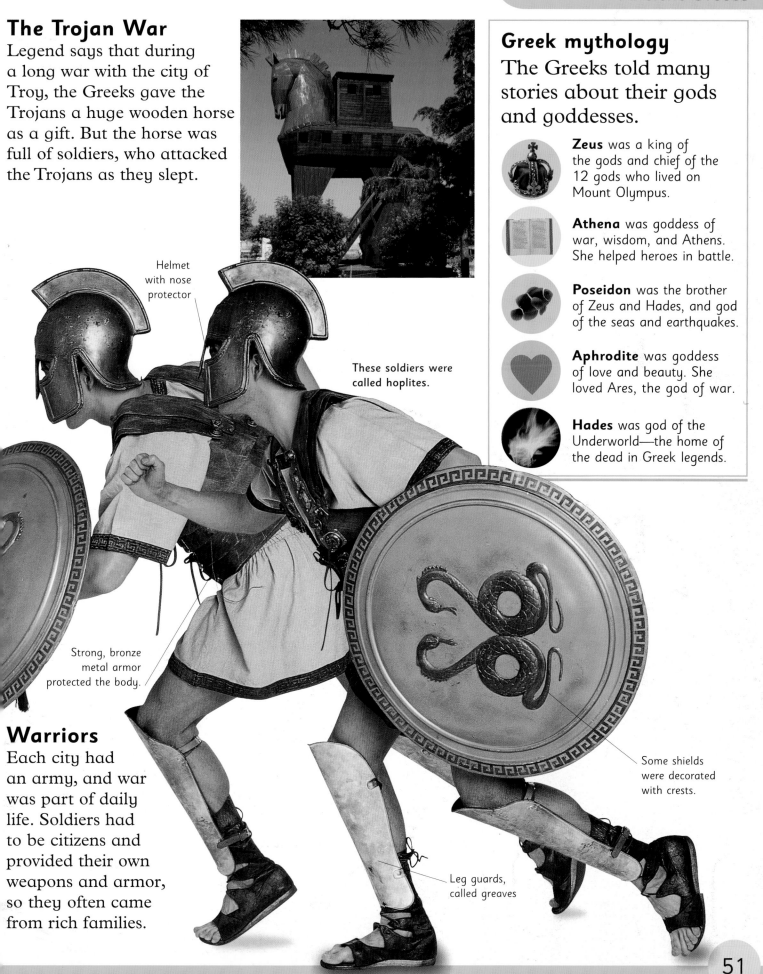

The Trojan War

Legend says that during a long war with the city of Troy, the Greeks gave the Trojans a huge wooden horse as a gift. But the horse was full of soldiers, who attacked the Trojans as they slept.

Greek mythology

The Greeks told many stories about their gods and goddesses.

Zeus was a king of the gods and chief of the 12 gods who lived on Mount Olympus.

Athena was goddess of war, wisdom, and Athens. She helped heroes in battle.

Poseidon was the brother of Zeus and Hades, and god of the seas and earthquakes.

Aphrodite was goddess of love and beauty. She loved Ares, the god of war.

Hades was god of the Underworld—the home of the dead in Greek legends.

Helmet with nose protector

These soldiers were called hoplites.

Strong, bronze metal armor protected the body.

Some shields were decorated with crests.

Leg guards, called greaves

Warriors

Each city had an army, and war was part of daily life. Soldiers had to be citizens and provided their own weapons and armor, so they often came from rich families.

The Romans

Ancient Rome began as a group of small villages along the Tiber River in Italy. It grew into a great and powerful city that ruled a mighty empire.

A Roman forum

The city of Rome

The city of Rome is still a busy place, just as it was in ancient times. If you visit Rome today, you can see the ruined Forum (ancient city center), the Colosseum, and many other buildings.

Gladiators

The Colosseum was a huge building in Rome where people went to watch wild beast shows and gladiator fights. Gladiators often fought to the death.

Lions and other wild animals were killed during the shows.

Gladiators were armed with nets and spears, or small shields and swords.

Up to 50,000 people could watch the fights in the arena.

What was a Roman villa?

Latin language

The Romans spoke a language called Latin. Roman children learned to write Latin by scratching letters on wooden boards that were covered in wax.

This inscription is written in Latin.

The Roman Empire

The Romans conquered a vast empire. They built this wall between Scotland and England to protect the boundary of their empire.

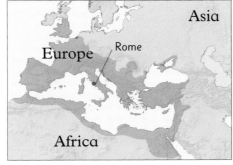

The purple area on this map shows the size of the Roman Empire in around 100 CE.

Hadrian's Wall

Famous Romans

Below, you can read about some of the most famous Romans.

Spartacus was a slave who led an army of slaves against the Romans.

Julius Caesar was a great general who ruled Rome. He was murdered.

Augustus was the first Roman emperor. After his death, he was made a god.

Ovid was a Roman poet. He wrote many poems about myths and legends.

Emperor Hadrian toured the empire and built walls and forts to guard it.

The Roman army

The Romans had the best army in the world. Their soldiers conquered many countries and guarded the empire. The soldiers often had to march long distances.

A standard (army flag)

A soldier's sandals

Roman roads

In peacetime, Roman soldiers were kept busy building roads. Roads were important for moving the army around the empire. Roman roads were usually very straight. Some are still used today.

53

A large house in the countryside.

The Vikings

The Vikings lived more than 1,000 years ago. Their home was in Scandinavia, in northern Europe, but they are famous for their long sea journeys to distant lands.

Mast

The sail was made from wool or linen.

Ropes

Longships

Viking boats were called longships. They were built from wood, and were fast and strong enough to cover vast distances. A longship carried about 80 Vikings, who rowed and sailed the ship.

Important Vikings were buried in their longships.

Viking travelers

The Vikings were daring sailors and explorers. They made fierce raids on the countries of western Europe. They went in search of trade and new lands to live in—even as far away as North America.

Scandinavia

Atlantic Ocean

Europe

North America

The Vikings reached North America in about the year 1000 CE.

Turn and learn

30-31 Writing and printing
60-61 Explorers
114-115 Ships and boats

What is the Viking alphabet called?

Warrior duty

Most Vikings were farmers, but they had to be ready to fight at a moment's notice. They always kept their weapons and armor close by.

Viking houses were usually built of stone or wood.

Viking homes

Viking families lived in houses made from wood, stone, or turf. An opening was made in the roof to let out smoke from the cooking fire. People sat on stools or benches around the fire and slept on raised beds.

Spear made of iron and wood

Viking warriors carried wooden shields and wore armor made from leather or chain mail.

Padded leather tunic

Helmet with noseguard

Chain-mail shirt

Round wooden shield

Long wool socks

Goat-skin shoes

Iron sword

Swords and spears were used for fighting.

A small statue of a Viking god called Freyr

Storytelling

To entertain each other, the Vikings told long stories about their heroes, gods, and great warriors. The stories were called sagas.

Runes

The Vikings carved poems and inscriptions using symbols called runes. Runes were mostly made of straight lines, so it was easy to carve them on wood or stone.

Runes

It is called "Futhark" ("foo-thark").

Aztecs, Incas, and Mayas

Three great civilizations grew up in the ancient Americas. They were called the Aztecs, Mayas, and Incas. These people built great cities and temples to their gods.

Aztec warrior's headdress

Where did they live?
The Mayas lived in Central America, while the Aztecs ruled most of Mexico. The Inca Empire was on the west coast of South America.

Pyramid of the Moon at Teotihuacan

Pyramid temple
Both the Aztecs and the Mayas had pyramid-shaped temples, with long flights of steps leading to a shrine on top. Here their priests sacrificed captives as offerings to the gods.

Chicomecoatl, the Aztec goddess of corn

Gods and farming
The Aztecs prayed to the gods to make their crops grow. Most important crop was corn. It was ground into flour for making flat breads called tortillas.

How were the Incas like the ancient Egyptians?

Spanish galleon

Spanish invasion

In the 16th century, Spanish explorers came to the Americas. Their arrival meant the end of the Aztec, Maya, and Inca civilizations. Many people were killed and their cities destroyed.

Inca gold

The Incas made objects from gold. The Spanish greed for gold led to the end of the Inca Empire.

Llamas were important to the Incas. They provided wool and transportation.

Gold armbands may have been worn by the bravest Inca warriors.

Statues of Inca gods were made from gold to show honor toward them.

Mayan cities

The Maya built great cities, filled with magnificent stone temples, palaces, and squares. This is the Temple of the Great Jaguar in the Mayan city of Tikal.

Tikal in Guatemala, Central America

hands on

Make an Aztec headdress from cardboard. Cut a cardboard circle to fit your head. Glue on cardboard feathers. Paint it and tape the ends together.

Inca farmers

This is the Inca city of Machu Picchu, located high in the Andes Mountains in Peru. Farmers grew crops in level fields cut into the mountainside. Corn, legumes (beans), and squash were their main crops.

Ruins of Machu Picchu's buildings can still be seen in Peru today.

They made mummies.

Knights and castles

Even for brave knights, attacking a castle was dangerous. Thick walls kept them out, and the castle archers had their bows and arrows at the ready.

Types of castle

The first castles were made from wood, but stone was stronger.

Early castles were strong, square keeps (towers) built of stone.

French castles (châteaux) were defended by lofty towers and moats.

Japanese castles were built by warrior lords and had decorative roofs.

The **Red Fort** in India was a palace with stone walls 100 ft (30 m) tall.

Castle design

Massive walls and towers made castles almost impossible for enemy soldiers to attack. Many castles were built on hills, so they were difficult to reach.

Battlements

Tower

Thick walls

hands on

Make a knight's shield from a big piece of colored posterboard. Decorate the shield with your own coat of arms, cut out of silver paper.

Jousting

In peacetime, knights fought practice battles, called jousts, to train for war. They used poles (lances) to knock each other off their horses.

What was chain mail?

Helmet

Knights
Knights were soldiers who fought on horseback. They wore heavy armor made from iron and were armed with axes, swords, and maces (clubs).

Mace

A knight used his sword to stab between the gaps in an enemy's armor.

Leg guard (greave)

Spur

Buffalo horns

Samurai warriors wore armor made from coated wood or plates of metal laced together.

Samurai warriors
In Japan, knights were called samurai. They were warriors who fought for a powerful lord and followed a strict code of honor.

Leather leg protector

Samurai sword

Archers aimed arrows from the walls at their attackers.

Lance

Each knight had his own pattern, called his coat of arms.

Shield

Moat

Armor made from small loops of metal.

Explorers

For thousands of years, people have set out to explore far-off places. Some explorers hoped to find new lands or goods to trade. Others wanted an adventure.

Early explorers
Thousands of years ago, people called the Polynesians explored the vast Pacific Ocean. They sailed in fragile canoes like this one and settled on the Pacific islands. Such canoes would have had sails.

Great expeditions
These are some of the greatest and most daring explorers.

Marco Polo traveled overland from Italy to China in the 13th century.

Burke and **Wills** were the first to cross Australia from south to north in 1860.

Lewis and **Clark** traveled across the US from east to west in 1804–1806.

Magellan led the first mission to sail around the world in the 16th century.

The *Santa María* was the leading ship of Columbus's expedition.

Columbus's other two ships were called the *Niña* and the *Pinta*.

Christopher Columbus
In August 1492, Christopher Columbus set out from Spain, hoping to sail to Asia. In October, he saw land, but it was not Asia. Columbus had reached the new world of the Americas.

Which Italian explorer is America named after?

Mount Everest

In May 1953, Edmund Hillary and Tenzing Norgay became the first people to climb to the top of Mount Everest, the highest mountain on Earth.

The South Pole

The first person to reach the icy South Pole was the Norwegian explorer Roald Amundsen, in December 1911. He beat a rival British expedition, led by Captain Robert Scott, by just a month.

Amundsen and one of his team taking photographs at the South Pole in 1911

This hood was worn by the Anglo-Irish explorer Ernest Shackleton on his attempt to reach the South Pole in 1907–08.

This equipment is from Captain Scott's expedition.

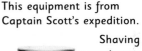

Knife

Shaving mirror

Mug

Matches

Exploring the deep

Scientists use submersibles (small submarines) to explore the ocean floor and look for sunken ships. They have discovered features and animals never seen before.

The *Santa María*

Amerigo Vespucci.

20th century

The 20th century was the time from 1901 to 2000. In the 20th century, there were many events, inventions, and discoveries that changed people's lives forever.

British air force symbol

A British fighter aircraft from World War II

World wars

There were two world wars during the 20th century. World War I lasted from 1914 to 1918. World War II lasted from 1939 to 1945. Millions of soldiers and civilians died in these wars.

Nuclear power

The first nuclear power plant was opened in 1954. Today, there are about 400 of them in the world. While they provide energy, these power plants also produce dangerous waste.

Nearly three quarters of France's electricity is made at nuclear power plants. This one is on the Seine River.

This is *Sirius*, a ship owned and used by the Greenpeace organization.

The tracks stop the heavy tank from sinking into mud.

Tank

Thick armor protects the crew of the tank.

Who was the first person to go into space? And when?

Popular music

The Beatles were one of the most successful rock groups of all time. In the 1960s, millions of people bought their records. Performances on television also helped to boost their fame. The Beatles split up in 1970.

Live telecast of a Beatles performance in New York

Man on the Moon

In 1969, astronauts visited the Moon for the first time. People all around the world watched on television as the US astronauts stepped onto the Moon's gray, dusty surface.

Buzz Aldrin

Buzz Aldrin was the second man on the Moon; Neil Armstrong was the first.

Space suit

The environment

Some people began to worry about the damage that humans are doing to the environment. They formed organizations such as Greenpeace and Friends of the Earth.

Nelson Mandela

There were many important political changes during the 20th century. Nelson Mandela fought against an unfair political system in South Africa. He became president of South Africa in 1994.

Advances

Advances made in the 20th century made many people's lives easier.

Mobile telephones and the **Internet** make it easy to keep in touch.

Medical advances help us to fight diseases and recover from injuries.

Inventions such as the jet engine have made travel fast and cheap.

Sports became extremely popular, and many sports people became very famous.

Scientific discoveries, such as DNA, helped medicine and technology.

A microchip is a set of circuits on a small plate through which electricity flows.

Technology

Many new types of technology were developed in the 20th century. Microchips were invented in the 1950s. They are used in computers, televisions, stereos, and many other machines.

A Russian cosmonaut (astronaut) named Yuri Gagarin. In 1961.

World of life

Anything living, such as plants and animals, makes up the living world. It is the world that is all around you—an amazing place to be.

Plants

Plants range from brightly colored flowers to massive trees. Plants keep us alive. Without plants, we would have nothing to eat and no oxygen to breathe.

Animals can be big and furry...

Many plants grow flowers with bright colors and sweet smells.

Bluebells

Brown bear

Fly agaric toadstools

Fungi

Mushrooms and toadstools are fungi. Fungi are not animals or plants—they are a separate group of living thing. Never pick fungi to eat—some are poisonous.

Animals

Animals are different from plants because they have to find their own food. Plants can make their own food. Some animals eat plants, and some eat other animals.

Brown bears belong to a group of animal called mammals. They weigh 1,100 lb (500 kg) and are very strong.

Humans

You are a type of animal, too—an animal called a human. There are billions of humans in the world, but there is no one quite like you.

...or small and delicate.

Blue morpho butterfly

Bears use their strong claws to dig up roots and to hunt for other animals to eat.

Picture detective

Look through the Living World pages and see if you can identify each of the picture clues below.

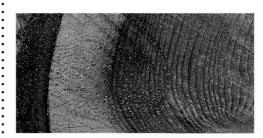

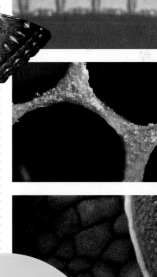

Turn and learn

14-15 Rain forests
98-99 Energy
124-125 Our planet
134-135 Water

A grizzly bear is a type of brown bear.

Plant life

The world is home to more than 350,000 different kinds of plant, from tiny pond plants to towering trees.

Fresh air
Plants take in a gas called carbon dioxide, which they use to make their food (see p. 70). They give off a gas called oxygen, which humans and other animals need to breathe.

Flowering plants
Some plants grow colorful flowers. The flower part is important, as it produces the seeds needed to grow new plants.

Plant life keeps the planet healthy.

Flower

Petal

Bees and other insects eat sugary nectar from flowers. They help to carry pollen from plant to plant.

Leaf

Which flower stinks of rotting meat?

Making seeds

Plants make seeds so that new plants can grow.

Petals are the bright parts of a flower. They attract insects and animals that carry pollen.

Pollen is the yellow, dusty stuff that seeds grow from. It is carried from one plant to another.

Seeds travel on animals, water, and the wind to reach the places where they will grow into new plants.

Meat-eating plants

The Venus flytrap is a plant that eats meat. It traps insects inside its spiked leaves and turns them into liquid food.

Cactus plants

Cacti grow in hot, dry deserts. They store water in their thick, stubby stems and use it to grow. Because of their prickly spines, very few animals are able to eat cacti.

Water-based plants

Some plants live in water. Water lily flowers and leaves float on the pond surface, while their roots grow in mud underwater.

Growing

Seeds grow once they reach the earth. A root grows downward into the soil, and a shoot grows up toward the sunlight.

Plants use their roots to suck up water and food from the soil.

Damselfly

Venus flytrap

hands on

Make a miniature garden inside a jar or can. Fill it with soil, then plant some seeds. Water them well and watch them grow.

The leaves snap shut if an insect touches them.

Stem

Leaf

67

The giant rafflesia. It is also the world's biggest flower.

Trees and forests

A tree is a plant with a thick, woody stem called a trunk. Some trees grow in huge groups, called forests. Forests grow all over the world.

Leaves from broad-leaved trees come in different shapes and sizes.

Beech

Oak

Maple

A forest in Scotland during the fall

Palm fronds

Broad-leaved trees

Oaks, maples, and beech trees have wide, flat leaves. In fall, the leaves turn yellow, red, or golden-brown, like the ones shown above. These trees lose their leaves in winter.

This giant tree has been hollowed out so that cars can drive through it.

Record-breaking trees

The tallest trees are coastal redwoods, like the one shown here from California. They grow to more than 360 ft (110 m) tall.

Turn and learn

14-15 Rain forests
134-135 Water
138-139 Climate and seasons

What is the oldest tree in the world?

Conifers

Conifers, such as pine and fir trees, are trees that have needles and cones instead of broad leaves and fruits. Many grow in the colder parts of the world.

A fir tree branch with needles

Brown fir cones

A conifer forest in winter

The trunk of a tree is made from tough, hard wood.

Palm trees

Palm trees have tall, skinny trunks that bend and sway in the wind. They have huge, fringed leaves called fronds. Palm trees usually grow in warm places.

Growth rings

The trunk is covered in a layer of bark.

People drink the liquid inside and eat the white parts.

A coconut

You can count a tree's growth rings to see how old it is.

Useful trees

Many useful things come from trees. Rubber comes from rubber trees. Dates and coconuts grow on palm trees. The paper used to make this book came from conifer trees.

A spruce tree that is almost 10,000 years old.

Plants and food

How many plants have you eaten today? Animals, including people, rely on plants for food because plants can make their own food from air, water, and sunlight.

Air

Water

Sunlight

Food for plants
Plants take water from the soil and a gas called carbon dioxide from the air. They use sunlight to turn the water and gas into sugary food. This process is called photosynthesis.

The food chain
Plants use food to grow. People and animals need food, too, but they cannot make their own. So they eat plants, things made from plants, or animals that eat plants.

Juicy fruits
When you munch a juicy apple, you are eating the fruit of an apple tree. The apple's tasty flesh grows around its seeds. Can you think of any other types of fruit that are good to eat?

Apple seeds

Is a tomato a fruit or a vegetable?

Plants we eat

Here are some of the plants, or parts of plants, that we eat every day.

Plant seeds can be good to eat. These are sunflower seeds.

Beans and **peas** are types of plant seed that we eat as vegetables.

Leaves and **stems**, such as cabbage, lettuce, and celery, are eaten by us.

Tubers, such as potatoes, and **roots**, such as carrots, grow underground.

Nuts are another type of plant seed. Some grow inside tough, hard shells.

Fruits, such as apples and oranges, have seeds inside. Many are healthy to eat.

Farming

All over the world, people grow plants to eat on farms and in gardens. This is a wheat field. A tractor is plowing the field to make the ground ready for the wheat seeds to be sown.

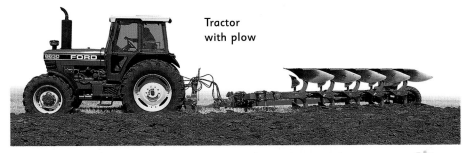

Tractor with plow

Grains of rice

Planting crops

In some places, crops are still planted and picked by hand. These farmers in Thailand are planting rice in a paddy field. Most types of rice need plenty of water to grow.

Turn and learn

42-43 Working people
90-91 Eating and digestion
98-99 Energy

A loaf of whole wheat bread

Harvesting crops

This machine is called a combine harvester. As it moves along, it collects the wheat stalks. Inside, the wheat is beaten around to separate the grain from the stalks.

It is a fruit, because it grows around the seeds.

Animal groups

There are more than a million types of animal. To make them easier to study, they are divided into groups.

Tiger

Rainbow lorikeet

Birds

Birds are animals with feathers and wings, although not all birds can fly. Baby birds hatch from hard-shelled eggs, which are often laid in a nest.

Snakes, such as this rattlesnake, are a type of reptile.

Reptiles

Reptiles are animals with dry, scaly skins that live mainly on land. Most baby reptiles hatch from leathery-shelled eggs, although some reptiles give birth to live young.

Tree frog

Amphibians

Amphibians are animals that live both in water and on land. They have damp, slimy skins and lay jellylike eggs. Frogs are amphibians.

What is the biggest animal ever?

Lion

Mammals

Mammals are animals that mostly give birth to live young and feed their babies on milk. Most mammals have fur or hair on their bodies.

Lions are mammals. Male lions grow bushy manes, which make them look bigger and fiercer.

Common fly

Insects

Insects, such as flies, are animals with six legs and bodies divided into three parts. Insects are the biggest group of animal; they can live almost anywhere.

Clownfish

Fish

Fish are animals that live in water and breathe through gills. They use their fins to swim. Fish live in oceans, seas, lakes, rivers, and ponds.

Picture detective

Look through the Living World pages and see if you can identify each of the picture clues below.

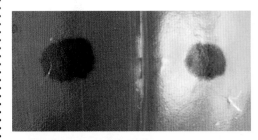

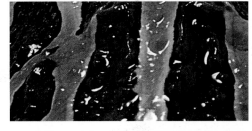

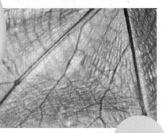

Turn and learn

12-13 Grasslands
86-87 Dinosaurs
134-135 Water
138-139 Climate and seasons

The blue whale.

Mammals

Mammals are animals with hair or fur on their bodies. They feed their babies on milk. Elephants, bats, whales, wolves, and humans are all mammals.

Once born, mammal babies feed on their mother's milk.

Mammal babies

Most mammals, such as monkeys, cats, and dogs, give birth to live young, which look like their parents. The babies grow inside their mothers' bodies until they are born.

Eastern gray kangaroo and joey

Even when older, a joey (young kangaroo) may jump into its mother's pouch for safety.

Mammals with pouches

Some mammals, such as kangaroos and koalas, have pouches on their bellies. Tiny baby kangaroos crawl into their mother's pouch to feed on milk and grow.

Mother and baby gorilla

74

Sea mammals

Whales, dolphins, and seals are mammals that live in the ocean. They have sleek bodies for swimming and flippers instead of arms and legs. They come to the surface to breathe the air.

Humpback whales

Flying mammals

Bats swoop through the air, looking for insects and fruits to eat. A bat's wings are made from leathery skin stretched across its long fingers.

A young human

Furry body

Primates

Mammals such as monkeys, apes, and human beings are called primates. There are lots of different types of monkey, but the only types of ape are chimpanzees, gorillas, orangutans, and gibbons.

A hibernating dormouse

Hibernation

Some mammals sleep all through winter, when it is cold and there is not much to eat. This is hibernation. When spring comes, they wake up to search for food.

Fur coats

Many mammals have fur coats for warmth and for camouflage (hiding).

An **arctic fox's** coat turns white in winter to hide it in ice and snow.

Cheetahs have spotted coats that make them hard to see as they stalk prey.

Yaks live high up on cold mountains. Thick, shaggy coats keep them warm.

A **zebra's** striped coat hides it in the herd, concealing it from lions.

A short-beaked echidna (spiny anteater) from Australia

Mammals that lay eggs

Spiny anteaters and duck-billed platypuses are very unusual mammals. Their babies hatch from eggs. Spiny anteaters lay their eggs in tiny pouches on their bellies. Platypuses lay their eggs in riverbank nests.

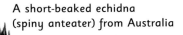

Echidna egg

The cheetah. It can sprint at more than 62 mph (100 kph).

Amphibians

Frogs, toads, newts, and salamanders are amphibians. Most kinds can live both in water and on land. They all have to be in water to lay their eggs.

This toad's patterned skin helps to hide it from enemies.

White's tree frog

Ornamental horned toad

Tadpole to frog
Baby frogs go through amazing changes before they become adults.

Frogspawn is the slimy, jellylike stuff laid by frogs. It is full of tiny black eggs.

Tadpoles hatch from the eggs. At first, they are just a round body and a long tail.

Small legs grow on the tadpoles and they start to look more like tiny frogs.

Baby frogs are ready to live on land. They leave the pond at a few weeks' old.

Frogs and toads
Frogs usually have smooth skin and long legs for leaping. Most toads have bumpy skin and shorter legs for crawling. This is how you can tell them apart.

European fire salamander

Newts and salamanders
Newts and salamanders are lizardlike amphibians. They have long bodies, long tails, and short legs. Some live on water, others on land. Some have brightly colored skin that shows they are poisonous.

Caecilians
This strange creature looks like a worm, but it is an amphibian. A caecilian uses its head to dig in the mud and find worms and insects to eat.

Common European frogs

Frogs have large, bulging eyes and good eyesight.

Which frog is the most poisonous?

With a well-timed hop, the frog leaps out of danger.

Northern
leopard frog

Leaping legs

Frogs are expert long jumpers. The champion is the African sharp-nosed frog, which can leap more than 16 ft (5 m) in a single hop. How far can you jump?

Forward-facing eyes enable tree frogs to handle a tricky climb.

Giant tree frog

Eating habits

Frogs and toads catch flying insects by flicking out their long, sticky tongues. They also eat worms, slugs, and snails— which they usually hunt at night.

Tree frogs have sticky toes to help them climb up the trees where they live.

hands on

Ask an adult to help you collect some frogspawn from a pond. Keep it in a large jar and watch the tadpoles hatch. Don't forget to put them back in the pond.

The golden poison-dart frog.

Reptiles

Reptiles can be tiny lizards or enormous snakes, many yards long. Reptiles mostly live in hot places because they need sunshine to keep their bodies warm.

Reptile groups

There are about 10,000 types of reptile alive today. They are split into different groups.

Lizards, such as this frilled lizard, which lives in Australia.

Tortoises and **turtles**, such as this leopard tortoise from Africa.

Crocodiles and **alligators**, such as this American alligator.

Snakes, such as this common milksnake from the Americas.

Reptile features

Reptiles come in many shapes and sizes, but they all have scaly skins. They run, walk, slither, and swim. Most reptiles lay eggs, which hatch on land.

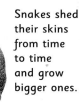

Snakes shed their skins from time to time and grow bigger ones.

Emerald tree boa

Record-breaking reptiles

The Komodo dragon (above) is the largest, heaviest lizard. The world's biggest reptile is the massive saltwater crocodile. It can grow to 23 ft (7 m) long and is extremely dangerous.

Hatching from eggs

Most reptiles lay eggs with leathery shells, which the babies hatch from. Here you can see a young leopard tortoise hatching from its egg. It takes two days for it to push its way out.

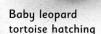
Baby leopard tortoise hatching

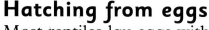

78

Meat-eaters

Crocodiles and alligators are fierce hunters. They hide underwater, then grab their prey with their sharp, pointed teeth. They eat fish, turtles, birds, and mammals.

Crocodiles grow up to 80 teeth.

Nile crocodile

Long lives

Some reptiles live for longer than most other animals. Tortoises can live for more than 100 years. You can tell their age from the patterns of rings on their shells.

Turn and learn

10-11 Deserts
86-87 Dinosaurs
102-103 Light and color

Color change

Many reptiles have green or brown skins to help them hide in the trees or on the ground. Chameleons can even change color, making them very difficult to see.

The chameleon can swivel its eyes to look behind itself.

Chameleons can be brown, green, or yellow— and all the shades in between.

Oustalet's chameleon

The reticulated python. It can grow to 33 ft (10 m) long.

Fish

Fish live in salty oceans and in rivers, lakes, and ponds. The whale shark is the biggest type of fish, and the tiny dwarf goby fish is the smallest.

Fish features

Most fish have scaly skins and fins for swimming through the water. They use gills for breathing underwater. Most fish lay lots of jellylike eggs, which baby fish hatch from.

Smooth body for moving through water

Back fin

Eye

Gills

Tail fin

Scaly skin

Seahorse fathers

Male seahorses are good fathers. The female squirts her eggs into a pouch on the male's belly. A few weeks later, the eggs hatch and the baby seahorses swim away.

Turn and learn

8-9 Seas and oceans
16-17 Rivers and lakes
134-135 Water

Male seahorse

Baby seahorses

Flatfish

Flatfish, such as sole and plaice, start off as normal fish shapes. Then their bodies flatten out and both eyes move to the same side of their heads. Their shape helps to hide them from enemies as they lie on the seabed.

How small is the dwarf goby fish?

Self defense

Fish are food for sharks and other sea hunters. Many tricks and features help fish to scare away their enemies.

Porcupine fish (or **pufferfish**) blow themselves up like prickly balloons to keep from being eaten.

Stingrays have needle-sharp spikes on their tails, which they whip around to sting enemies.

Stonefish look like harmless stones or rocks sitting on the seabed, but they are deadly poisonous.

Bony fish

Most fish have bony skeletons, just like humans do. Some bony fish swim around in huge groups, called schools. Being part of a crowd helps to hide them from enemies.

A school of fish

A shark's sharp teeth can be longer than your fingers.

Sharks can grow new teeth every few weeks.

Sharks and rays

Sharks and rays have skeletons made from tough, flexible cartilage, not bone. It is like the stuff you have in the tip of your nose. Sharks are the fiercest ocean hunters, but very few sharks will attack and eat people.

Smaller than your fingernail.

Birds

Birds live all over the world. Parrots and toucans live in the warm and wet rain forests. Penguins are at home in icy Antarctica. Birds like robins and thrushes are familiar backyard visitors.

Flying birds

Some birds fly long distances to find food and places to nest. The Arctic tern is a champion flier. Each year it flies from the Arctic to the Antarctic, and back again—a trip of 25,000 miles (40,000 km)!

Owls can fly silently through the night.

Huge eyes

Barn owl in flight

Long flight feathers

Bird features

All birds have wings and most birds can fly, although not all of them. Birds are the only animals with feathers. Their babies hatch from hard-shelled eggs, often laid in nests.

Long, strong wings

Sharp, hooked beak

Sharp claws for grabbing animal prey

Colorful male frigate bird

Feathers

Feathers keep birds warm and help them to fly. Some feathers are plain brown for camouflage. Others are very colorful and help the bird to attract a mate. Males are often very brightly colored.

Which birds make their nests from mud and spit?

Birds have hollow bones, which keep their bodies light for flying.

Night hunters

Some birds, such as this owl, hunt at night. Owls have huge eyes and sharp, sensitive hearing to help them find their prey in the dark. They feed on small mammals and birds.

Stiff tail feathers

Ostrich eggs weigh more than 3½ lb (1½ kg). Hummingbird eggs are just ½ in (1 cm) long.

Ostrich egg

Hummingbird egg

Biggest and smallest

Ostriches are the biggest birds in the world. They cannot fly, but they can run very fast. The smallest birds are hummingbirds, which are excellent fliers.

Beaks and bills

Birds use their beaks, or bills, for all kinds of jobs. They use them for feeding, cleaning their feathers, making a nest, and fighting off enemies.

Eagles have sharp, curved beaks for grabbing their prey and tearing it to pieces.

Pelicans have large, pouchlike beaks for scooping up and storing fish.

Parrots use their short, hooked beaks to grasp and tear up fruit, seeds, and nuts.

Toucan beaks are useful for reaching fruits that are hidden among the leaves.

Eggs and nests

Most birds lay their eggs in nests. They sit on the eggs to keep them warm until they hatch. Baby birds have no wing feathers and cannot fly. The parent birds bring food for them.

Nest of baby bluetits

The chicks stay in the nest until old enough to fly out and find food for themselves.

Insects and spiders

Insects and spiders live all over the world. There are more than a million types of insect—more than all other animal types put together.

Jeweled frog beetle

Head

Thorax

Abdomen

Wing

One of six legs

Insect features

An insect has six legs. Its body is divided into three parts, called the head, thorax, and abdomen. Its body is sometimes covered in a hard case. Many insects also have wings.

Adult ants are fast movers, but most do not have wings and cannot fly.

Ants

Insect workers

Hundreds of honeybees live in a home called a hive. Some of the bees are the "workers." They collect sweet nectar from flowers for making honey.

Types of insect

Most insects are very small, but they come in a wide range of shapes and colors. Grasshoppers, moths, flies, ants, and bees are all types of insect.

A ladybug's bright colors warn birds that it is not good to eat.

Which insects sing to each other?

Butterfly life cycle

Many insects, such as the European swallowtail butterfly, go through many changes as they grow.

Eggs are laid by the female on a leaf. They hatch into caterpillars.

The **caterpillar** feeds on the leaf and grows bigger.

The caterpillar makes a **chrysalis**. Inside, it turns into a butterfly.

The chrysalis splits open and the **adult**, the butterfly, finds its way out.

Spider features

It is easy to tell insects and spiders apart. A spider has eight legs, instead of six. Its body is divided into two parts, not three.

A spider's head and thorax are joined together.

One of eight legs

Red-kneed tarantula

Spinning webs

Many spiders spin webs from silk and use them to catch their supper. Any insect that flies into the web gets caught in the sticky silk. Then the spider pounces.

Spider relations

They might look very different, but scorpions, ticks, and mites are closely related to spiders. Some scorpions have a deadly sting at the tips of their tails.

Sting

Scorpion

European swallowtail butterfly

Slug

Millipede

Little creatures

These creepy-crawlies look like insects, but they are not. Can you see why? Do they have six legs, three parts to their bodies, or wings?

The eye-shaped markings on this butterfly's wings scare off hungry predators.

Earthworm

Wood lice

Centipede

Dinosaurs

Dinosaurs were reptiles that lived on Earth from about 225 to 65 million years ago. We know what they looked like from fossils.

Meat-eaters

Some dinosaurs killed other animals to eat. The terrifying *Tyrannosaurus rex* had massive jaws lined with daggerlike teeth for ripping apart its prey.

Dinosaur dates

Scientists divide the time when the dinosaurs lived into these three periods.

Dinosaurs such as this *Herrerasaurus* lived in the **Triassic period** (250 to 208 million years ago).

Dinosaurs such as this *Stegosaurus* lived in the **Jurassic period** (208 to 146 million years ago).

Dinosaurs such as this *Iguanodon* lived in the **Cretaceous period** (146 to 65 million years ago).

What does the word "dinosaur" mean?

Troodon

Egg shells

Dinosaur babies

Dinosaurs laid eggs. Some female dinosaurs made nests for their eggs and looked after their young when they hatched. These little dinosaurs are *Troodons*, which have just hatched out from their eggs.

Brachiosaurus used its long neck to reach leaves high up in the trees.

Plant-eaters

Many of the largest dinosaurs ate plants. Giants like this plant-eating *Brachiosaurus* weighed as much as 12 elephants.

Brachiosaurus

Stegosaurus

Smallest brain

Stegosaurus was a plant-eating dinosaur that grew up to 29 ft (9 m) long. But the brain of this elephant-sized giant was no bigger than a dog's.

Terrible lizard.

Dinosaur features

Many plant-eating dinosaurs had special features to protect themselves from hungry meat-eaters. Hunters used deadly disguises to help them sneak up on their prey.

Styracosaurus used its long nose horn to charge at enemies.

Hypsilophodon may have had camouflage, which helped it to hide.

Corythosaurus may have used its head crest to scare off rival males.

Death of the dinosaurs

About 65 million years ago, the dinosaurs died out. Some experts think that they starved to death after a giant meteorite hit the Earth.

This huge crater was made by a meteorite that hit the Earth.

Human body

Look in the mirror. What can you see? You see your body. Your body is an amazing thing that can do a lot of things, such as running, jumping, and singing.

Everyone has different fingerprints because everyone is different.

Are your eyes blue, brown, green, or gray— or a mixture of two of these colors?

Hair grows from your skin. What color is your hair?

Your whole body is covered in skin. It is tough and waterproof.

Clothes help to keep us warm or cool.

Your skin and muscles help you make faces.

88

Where is your thickest skin?

Body map

Your body is made of many different parts. Each part has an important job to do. The parts work together to keep you alive and healthy.

Brain

Your brain controls your whole body. It sends messages along tracks, called nerves.

Spine

Your two lungs take oxygen from the air so that you can breathe.

Lung Lung

Skeleton

Your skeleton has more than 200 bones. It helps you to move about and holds your body in shape. Your bones also protect other body parts.

Kidneys

Arm muscles

Lots of tiny bones in your hands help you to write and pick things up.

Your blood

Your blood carries food and oxygen to all parts of your body.

The **heart** pumps blood all around your body through veins and arteries.

Red blood cells pick up oxygen, which the body needs, from your lungs.

White blood cells help your body to fight disease.

Platelets are tiny pieces of cells that plug up a wound.

Leg muscles

Leg bones

Foot bones

Picture detective

Look through the Living World pages and see if you can identify each of the picture clues below.

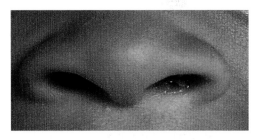

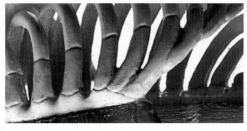

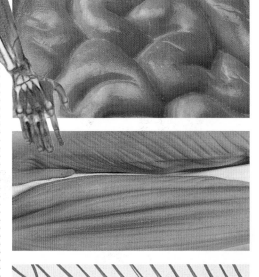

Turn and learn

64-65 World of life
98-99 Energy
134-135 Water

On the soles of your feet.

Eating and digestion

Your body needs food to keep it working. But before it can use the food, it breaks it into tiny pieces, which seep into your blood. This is called digestion.

Turn and learn

64-65 World of life
70-71 Plants and food
98-99 Energy

Mouth
In your mouth, your teeth chop up and chew your food. Your spit helps to break food down and makes it easy to swallow. When you swallow, your food goes down a tube in your throat and into your stomach.

Teeth

Tongue

Your food travels through your body...

This tube diagram is not the same shape as the tubes inside your body.

Stomach
Your stomach is like a stretchy bag that fills with food. Inside, your food is churned up and mixed with stomach juices. They break your food down into a thick souplike mixture.

This photograph of part of the stomach lining was taken through a microscope.

Why does your stomach rumble?

Intestines

Next, your food goes into long tubes called your intestines. It seeps through the walls of the intestines into your blood. Your blood takes the nutrients (goodness) in the food around your body.

Small intestine

This intestine is called your "small" intestine because it is narrow. In fact, it is as long as a bus!

You get rid of waste water and solid waste when you go to the bathroom.

Stomach

Small intestine

Large intestine

Getting rid of waste

Any waste food travels from your small intestine into your large intestine. It is stored there until you go to the bathroom and push it out as solid waste.

Your small and large intestines are coiled up inside your abdomen.

A meal takes about three days to pass all the way through your digestive system.

... along a series of pipes and tubes.

Your mouth, stomach, and intestines are called your digestive system.

A balanced diet

You need to eat a mixture of foods to keep you strong and healthy. This is called a balanced diet.

Carbohydrates, such as pasta, rice, and bread, give you lots of energy.

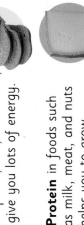

Protein in foods such as milk, meat, and nuts helps you to grow.

Vitamins in fruits and vegetables keep your body working properly.

Fiber in brown bread and vegetables keeps your digestive system working.

Fat in butter and cheese gives you energy. Too much fat is bad for you.

91

Muscles and movement

Your body can run, jump, skip, and hop. This is because the bones and muscles inside you work together to make your body move.

Skull

Your skeleton is made of more than 200 bones.

Ribs

Pelvis

The skeleton
There are hard, bumpy bones under your skin. They are joined together to make up the bony structure called your skeleton.

This skeleton shows how your bones move as you run.

Where are your smallest bones and muscles?

Your muscles

All over your skeleton are rubbery muscles. They are fixed to your bones by straps called tendons. Your muscles pull on your bones to make you move.

Making faces

Each time you make a face, you use lots of different muscles. There are more than 20 muscles in your face.

Smiling uses muscles to pull up the corners of your mouth.

Frowning uses muscles in your forehead to wrinkle it up.

Pulling this face uses a very special muscle—your tongue.

You have about 640 muscles. They make up about a third of your weight.

Your triceps muscle pulls on your arm bones to straighten your arm.

Many muscles pull on your bones, but some pull on your skin.

Your biceps muscle is long and relaxed.

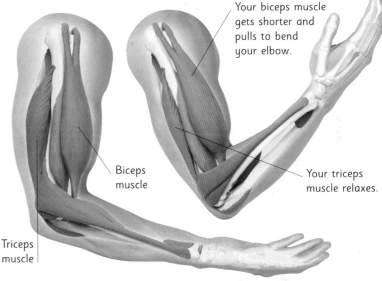

Your biceps muscle gets shorter and pulls to bend your elbow.

Biceps muscle

Triceps muscle

Your triceps muscle relaxes.

How muscles work

When you want to move your arm, your brain sends a message to your arm muscles. This tells them to get shorter. As they do, they pull on your arm bone and move it.

Muscle building

If you do plenty of exercise, you can make your muscles bigger. The biggest muscles in your body are in your bottom and the tops of your legs.

Special muscles

Some muscles do not make you move. Instead, they make you breathe and digest your food. Your heart is a special muscle that pumps blood around your body.

Blood vessel

The muscles in your heart never get tired or stop working.

Heart

93

Brain and senses

You use your brain to think.

Your brain is the part of your body that makes you think, feel, and remember. It makes sure that the rest of you works properly.

Your brain

Your brain is hidden inside your head. It looks a little bit like a soft, wrinkly lump of grayish-pink jelly.

Your hard, bony skull protects your brain from damage.

Nerves

Your brain is linked to your body by fibers called nerves. Nerves carry messages from your body to your brain and back again.

A bundle of nerves runs down your back, inside your backbone.

Your brain weighs about the same as 12 apples.

If you prick your finger, your brain makes you feel pain.

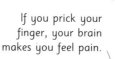

Reflex actions

If you accidentally prick your finger on a rose thorn, your brain quickly makes you pull your hand away. This fast reaction is called a reflex action.

Do smart people have bigger brains?

Your senses

You know what is happening around you by seeing, hearing, smelling, tasting, and touching things. These are called your senses.

Your eyes see the pictures, then your brain tells you what they are.

Eyes and seeing

Your eyes have special nerves that pick up light. They send messages to your brain, telling you what you are seeing.

Your ears pick up loud and soft sounds.

Different parts do different jobs.

Ears and hearing

Your ears catch sounds and send them deep inside your head. Nerves send messages about the sounds to your brain.

Nose and smelling

Nerves inside your nose tell you what you are smelling. Some things, such as this shoe, smell terrible. Other things smell nice!

Tongue and tasting

You taste with your tongue. It is covered with tiny bumps, called taste buds, that pick up tastes from your food.

Skin and touch

Nerves in your skin tell you if things feel hard, soft, hot, or cold. They also warn you of danger by making you feel pain.

Brown sugar   Grapes   Spaghetti

Can you tell what you are touching without looking?

No. Everyone's brain is about the same size.

World of science

Do you study science at school? Science helps us to understand the world around us. It also helps us to make medicines, grow more food, make new materials, and protect the environment.

Red blood cell

White blood cell

Blood cells seen through a microscope

A microscope lets a scientist examine very tiny things, such as blood cells.

Microscope

How scientists work

Scientists must work carefully and in a logical way. They write down how they think something works. This is called a theory. They do experiments (tests) to see if their theories (ideas) are correct.

Science experiments

During experiments scientists take measurements and carefully watch what happens. They write down their findings and decide whether the results prove their theory, or show anything interesting.

What is the name for a scientist who studies dinosaurs and fossils?

Theory of materials

An important scientific theory is that everything is made of very tiny particles.

 Solids hold their shape, because the particles are joined together.

 Liquids can flow, because the particles are only loosely joined.

 Gases fill any container, because the particles are free from each other.

Scientific theories

Scientists have tested thousands of theories about the world around us. In the 1660s, Isaac Newton wrote down a theory about why things fall downward—called the theory of gravity.

Gravity pulls everything down toward the Earth.

An apple falls downward because of gravity.

Gravity makes the apple fall faster and faster.

Gravity

Famous scientists

Some scientists are world famous because they have made amazing discoveries. Albert Einstein (1879–1955) is the most famous scientist of all. He wrote down theories that have helped us to understand the universe.

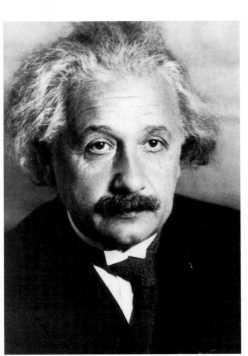
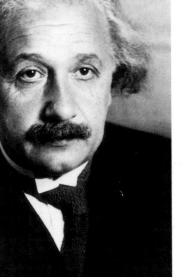

Albert Einstein was brilliant at physics and mathematics.

Picture detective

Look through the Science and Technology pages to identify each of the picture clues below.

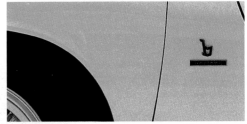

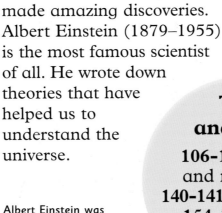
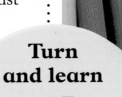

Turn and learn

106-107 Forces and movement
140-141 The universe
154-155 Space exploration

A paleontologist.

Energy

If you did not eat your meals, you would not have enough energy to play games, stay awake, or even think! Energy makes things happen, and nothing can take place without it.

A heavy roller coaster car has lots of movement energy.

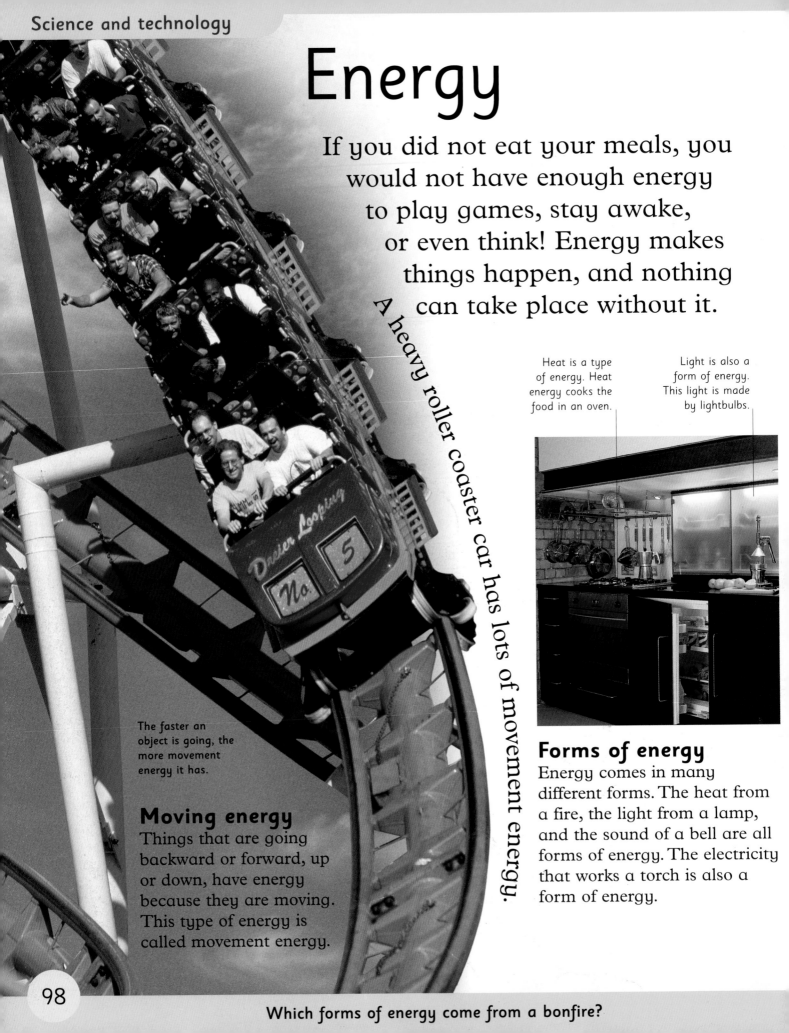

Heat is a type of energy. Heat energy cooks the food in an oven.

Light is also a form of energy. This light is made by lightbulbs.

The faster an object is going, the more movement energy it has.

Moving energy

Things that are going backward or forward, up or down, have energy because they are moving. This type of energy is called movement energy.

Forms of energy

Energy comes in many different forms. The heat from a fire, the light from a lamp, and the sound of a bell are all forms of energy. The electricity that works a torch is also a form of energy.

Which forms of energy come from a bonfire?

Fuels

Wood, gasoline, and coal are called fuels. They have energy in them. The energy in gasoline makes cars move along.

Filling a car with fuel is like filling it with energy.

Orange juice

Milk

Cereal

You can run a long way using the energy in your breakfast foods.

Apple

Nuts and raisins

Chocolate

Energy is stored in your body as fat.

Your muscles turn stored energy into movement.

Changing energy

Energy can change from one form to another. Here are some changes of energy that we use.

Electric motors change electrical energy into movement energy.

Lightbulbs change electrical energy into light energy.

Solar panels change light energy from the Sun into electrical energy.

Drums change movement energy (when you hit them) into sound energy.

Loudspeakers change electrical energy into sound energy.

Food as fuel

All these foods have energy stored in them, ready to be used. For example, an apple tree uses energy from sunlight to grow. Some of this energy is stored in its apples.

Stored energy

Food is fuel for your body. When we eat food, the energy gets stored in our bodies. The energy is released when we need it.

Saving energy

Keeping a house warm in winter uses lots of energy and is expensive. Fluffy insulation in the loft helps to stop heat energy from leaking away through the roof.

Heat energy, light energy, and sound energy.

Electricity

What happens when you switch on a light or turn on your computer? Electricity starts flowing and makes the light or the computer work.

Generating stations

Electricity is made at a generating station. Coal, gas, or oil are burned to make heat. Then the heat is turned into electricity. Electricity can also be generated through renewable sources, such as wind and water.

Electricity flows along this copper wire.

The plastic stops electricity escaping from the wire.

Power to your home

Electricity travels to your home along thick wires. Some wires hang on towers and some are hidden underground.

Electricity flows to your home along wires like these.

Conductors and insulators

Electrical cables are made of metal and plastic. The metal lets electricity flow. It is called a conductor. The plastic makes the cable safe to touch. It is called an insulator.

The wires hang from tall metal towers.

Electricity is very dangerous. Never poke anything into a socket.

What kind of electricity can you sometimes see in the sky?

Wires carry electricity from a battery to the electromagnet.

Iron bar

Electric magnets

A coil of wire with electricity flowing around it is called an electromagnet. It pulls on metal things, just like an ordinary magnet does. Motors have electromagnets inside them.

Iron filings

Wire is wrapped around the iron bar many times.

Making electricity

Electricity can be made from coal, gas, and oil, or from the sunlight, wind, and water around us.

 Hydroelectric dams use the power of flowing water to make electricity.

 Solar cells are used to turn the energy from sunlight into electricity.

 Wind turbines use the wind to power machines that make electricity.

 Wave generators turn the energy in powerful ocean waves into electricity.

Wire

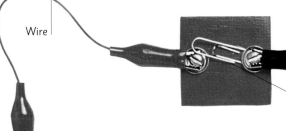

Closing the switch completes the circuit so that the electricity can flow.

The electricity flowing around this circuit comes from two batteries.

Electric circuits

An electric circuit is a loop that electricity can flow around. Electricity flows around this circuit to make the two bulbs light up.

Crocodile clip

Lightbulb

A lightbulb turns electricity into light.

 **hands on**
Rub a party balloon up and down on your clothes. The balloon will now stick to a wall. This happens because of a kind of electricity called static.

A battery is a store of electricity. It pushes electricity around the circuit.

Lightning (static electricity).

Light and color

Light is amazing. We can only see things because of the light that enters our eyes. Light comes in lots of beautiful colors.

Light rays

Light travels in straight lines, called rays. Light rays cannot go around corners. If something gets in the way, it blocks the light rays and makes a shadow.

The shadow is the same shape as the object that is blocking the light rays.

Shadow puppet

A shadow is a place where light does not reach.

You can see yourself in a mirror because light bounces off the glass.

This puppet is blocking the rays of light from the flashlight.

A flashlight casts dramatic shadows.

Flashlight

Bouncing light

We see things because light rays bounce off them and into our eyes. Then our eyes send signals to our brain and we see pictures.

Sources of light

Most of the light we see comes from the Sun. Lightbulbs, like the one in this flashlight, use electricity to make light.

What is the fastest thing in the universe?

Mixing colors

Mixing two different colors together makes a new color. You can make many different colors for a picture by mixing up just a few colors.

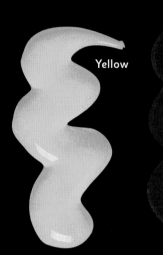

Red

Blue

Yellow

Red, yellow, and blue are called the primary colors.

Colors in light

Light from the Sun is made up of many different colors. When it rains you can see a rainbow, which contains lots of these different colors.

hands on

Try making a rainbow. Stand outside with your back to the Sun and spray water from a garden hose into the air. How many colors can you see?

Bending light

When light rays hit a glass surface, the glass makes them bend. A magnifying glass bends light to make things look bigger than they really are.

Magnifying glass

Blue morpho butterfly

The magnifying glass makes the butterfly's wing look much bigger.

Using colors

People, plants, and animals use colors in lots of different ways.

Red means danger. A red line around a sign means "look out"!

Green means "okay." A green light means it is safe to cross the road.

Yellow on this frog's skin means "don't eat me, I'm poisonous!"

Bright feathers help birds, such as this rainbow lorikeet, to attract a mate.

Colorful flowers attract insects and birds, which pollinate them.

103

Sound

Every day, we hear natural sounds, like the wind, and other noises such as cars and airplanes. We also put together different sounds to make music.

Sound waves

Sound levels

Loudness is measured in decibels. Very loud sounds can damage ears.

Falling leaves make a "rustling" sound of about 20 decibels.

Talking measures about 60 decibels. Whispering measures about 30.

Vacuum cleaners make noises of between 60 and 80 decibels.

Jet engines are very loud. An aircraft taking off measures 140 decibels.

Making sound

Sounds are made when things vibrate (move quickly back and forth). They make the air vibrate, too. The vibrations spread through the air in waves. We hear the sound when the waves enter our ears. How close we are to the noise affects how loud it seems.

Percussion instruments

Hitting a metal tray makes the tray vibrate.

Percussion instruments have parts that crash together.

Loud and quiet sounds

Big vibrations in the air have lots of energy. They sound very loud. Small vibrations in the air have much less energy. They sound very quiet.

A stringed instrument has vibrating strings.

The sound waves from the tray make the paper vibrate, which makes the sugar grains on it jump around.

What makes the strings of a violin vibrate?

A bat's large ears help it to listen for echoes.

Horseshoe bat

The speed of sound

Sound travels very fast. It goes at 750 mph (1,200 kph) through the air. Things that travel faster than sound are called supersonic. They cause the air to make a loud, booming noise called a sonic boom.

Bouncing sounds

Have you ever heard an echo? An echo is made when a sound bounces off a wall or a cliff face. You hear the sound twice. Bats send out high-pitched sounds and listen for their echoes to find prey.

Lockheed flies twice as fast as sound.

Lockheed Martin F-35 Lightning II is a fighter plane.

Wind instruments

A drum is a percussion instrument.

Turn and learn

34-35 Music
74-75 Mammals
82-83 Birds
94-95 Brain and senses

High and low sounds

Fast vibrations make noises that sound very high, such as a whistle. Slow vibrations make noises that sound low, such as a roar.

Animal sounds

Animals such as birds, dolphins, and dogs use sounds to communicate with each other. Some animals hear sounds that we cannot hear. Dogs can hear very high sounds.

A wind instrument makes sound using air that vibrates inside a tube.

A bow.

Forces and movement

A force is a push or a pull. When you pull (or push) on a door or on your school bag, or push on your bike's pedals (or its brakes) you are making forces.

Making things move

Forces can change the way things are moving. A force can make a thing start or stop, make it go faster or slower, or make it spin around.

Weighing machines work by measuring the pull of gravity on an object.

Gravity pulls the Moon toward the Earth. It stops the Moon drifting off into space.

Gravity and weight

When you jump in the air, you always fall back to the ground. The force that pulls you down is called gravity. Gravity pulls everything toward the Earth. The weight of something is the force that gravity pulls it down with.

Apple

This girl is swinging backward and forward because forces are pushing and pulling on her.

Why do things weigh less on the Moon than they do on the Earth?

Bending and stretching

Forces can also make things bend, stretch, and change shape. Pulling on the ends of a spring or rubber band makes it get longer. Pushing on the ends of a spring makes it shorter.

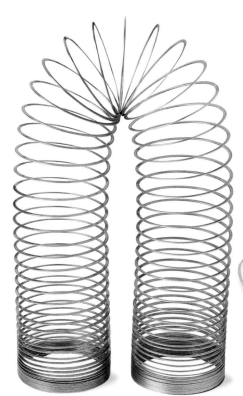

Metal coil

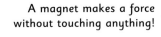

A magnet makes a force without touching anything!

This horseshoe magnet is pulling on steel objects.

Magnets

Magnets pull some metal things toward them. All magnets have two ends, called north and south poles. Two south poles, or two north poles, push each other away.

Forces help us to move things.

Pressure

Pressure is how much force pushes on a certain area of something. At the pointed end of this pin (above) the pressure is very high, so the point goes in. At the flat end, the pressure is much less.

There is a force called friction between your shoes and the ground. It stops your shoes from sliding along.

hands on

Try pulling on a rope tied to a tree. The harder you pull with a force, the harder the rope pulls back. Forces always work in pairs in this way.

Because the pull of gravity is weaker on the Moon.

Industry and invention

The food you eat, the bus you take
to school, and the fuel that heats your
home are all made by industries.
The machines and gadgets you
use were all invented by somebody.

A construction
worker on a
building site

Steel is used in
the construction
of buildings.

Big industries
Here are some of the
world's biggest industries.
They produce most of
the things we need.

Manufacturing industries
make all the machines and
gadgets that we use.

The **mining** industry digs
up coal and the rocks that
we get metals from.

Oil and **gas** industries
make oil and gas into
fuels and other products.

The **construction**
industry builds houses,
skyscrapers, bridges,
tunnels, and dams.

Food and
farming industries
produce crops, meat,
and ready-made meals.

Iron and steel industry
Iron and steel are very important
materials that many industries need.
Every year, millions of tons of iron
and steel are made from rocks
in the ground.

108

Communications inventions

The telephone, satellites, and the Internet are all inventions in communications. They make it easy for us to talk to each other.

The user spoke into the mouthpiece.

This is the earpiece where the user would listen.

Small, modern family car

Telephone from the 1920s

The engine under the hood is very powerful. New technology makes these engines less likely to go wrong.

Transportation inventions

Jet engines, diesel engines, and hovercraft are all inventions in transportation. They help us to travel quickly and safely from place to place.

The microprocessor

If the microprocessor had not been invented, we would not have personal computers, games consoles, smartphones, tablets, and many other electronic machines.

Microprocessors are tiny electronic circuits.

Picture detective

Look through the Science and Technology pages to identify each of the picture clues below.

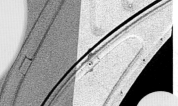

Turn and learn

46-47 Early people
130-131 Earth's materials
152-153 Space travel

Charles Babbage.

Cars, trucks, and trains

Cars, trucks, and trains are types of vehicle that carry people and goods all around the world. These moving machines travel around on roads and railroad tracks.

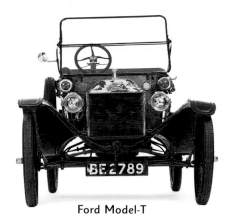
Ford Model-T

The first cars
The first cars were open topped and traveled at slow speeds. A man walked in front with a flag to warn people that a car was coming.

In this car, the engine is kept at the rear.

A car's engine is normally stored under the hood.

Metal body

Lamborghini Miura

Rubber tires grip the road.

Cars today
Modern cars have powerful engines to turn their wheels, and strong bodies made from metal. Every year, millions of new cars are built.

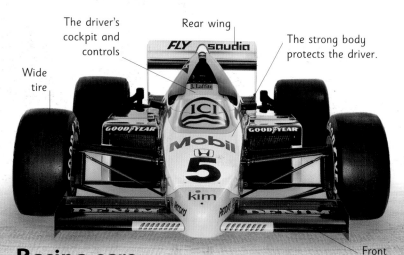

The driver's cockpit and controls

Rear wing

The strong body protects the driver.

Wide tire

Front wing

Racing cars
This racing car whizzes along at more than 186 mph (300 kph). Its large, rubber tires stop it from skidding as it speeds around corners.

110

Kinds of car

Cars come in all kinds of shapes and sizes. Here are some fun examples.

Classic cars are old makes of car. Some people collect them to display at shows.

Monster trucks are pickup trucks with huge tires as tall as an adult.

Limousines are luxury cars with big, comfy seats inside.

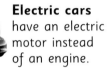
Electric cars have an electric motor instead of an engine.

High-speed Eurostar trains travel between Britain and Europe through the Channel Tunnel.

Trains

Trains move along on railroad tracks. The first trains had steam engines. Modern trains have electric motors or diesel engines.

This train was built more than 200 years ago to pull wagons in mines.

Driver's sleeping compartment

This trailer is called a curtain-sided trailer.

Big trucks

The biggest trucks are called articulated trucks. They have a tractor at the front and a trailer at the back, full of cargo.

Turn and learn

98-99 Energy
108-109 Industry and invention
116-117 Engineering

Lots of big tires spread out the truck's weight.

The Shanghai Maglev train in China. It has a top speed of 310 mph (500 kph).

Flying machines

Planes were only invented just over 100 years ago. Today, millions of people fly on planes every day to different places around the world.

The pilot steers the glider by moving a bar from side to side.

The wing is made of plastic fabric.

Strong harness

A hang-glider

Gliders

A glider is a plane with no engine. It glides on currents of rising air. This glider is called a hang-glider because the pilot hangs down from its wing.

Wright Flyer

The first plane

The first plane to fly was called the *Wright Flyer*. It was built in the US in 1903. The *Flyer* was a biplane, which means it had two sets of wings.

Jet engine

Emergency door

The fuselage is a strong metal tube.

Tail fin

Wing

Undercarriage

Which is the biggest airplane ever built?

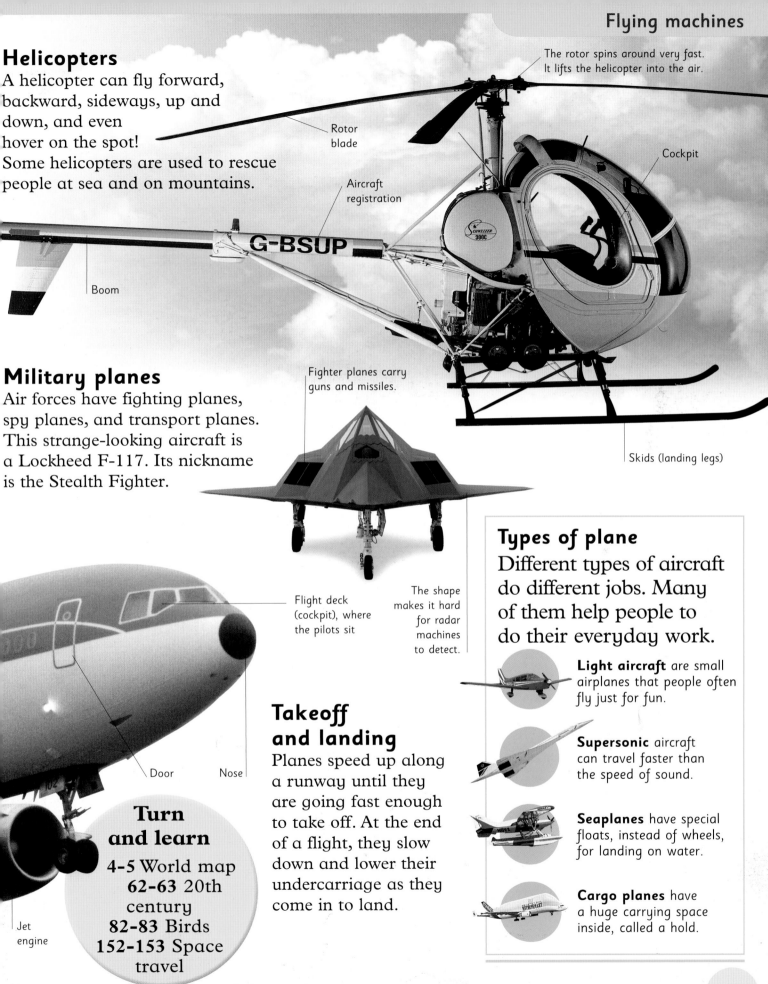

Helicopters

A helicopter can fly forward, backward, sideways, up and down, and even hover on the spot! Some helicopters are used to rescue people at sea and on mountains.

The rotor spins around very fast. It lifts the helicopter into the air.

Rotor blade

Cockpit

Aircraft registration

G-BSUP

Boom

Skids (landing legs)

Military planes

Air forces have fighting planes, spy planes, and transport planes. This strange-looking aircraft is a Lockheed F-117. Its nickname is the Stealth Fighter.

Fighter planes carry guns and missiles.

Flight deck (cockpit), where the pilots sit

The shape makes it hard for radar machines to detect.

Door   Nose

Jet engine

Turn and learn

4-5 World map
62-63 20th century
82-83 Birds
152-153 Space travel

Takeoff and landing

Planes speed up along a runway until they are going fast enough to take off. At the end of a flight, they slow down and lower their undercarriage as they come in to land.

Types of plane

Different types of aircraft do different jobs. Many of them help people to do their everyday work.

Light aircraft are small airplanes that people often fly just for fun.

Supersonic aircraft can travel faster than the speed of sound.

Seaplanes have special floats, instead of wheels, for landing on water.

Cargo planes have a huge carrying space inside, called a hold.

113

The Antonov An-225 (or "Mriya"). It has a maximum takeoff weight of 600 tons.

The crew controls the ship from a room called the bridge.

Ships and boats

Have you been across the sea on a ferry or an ocean liner? Ferries and liners are called ships. Most ships carry cargo. Boats are like ships, but they are smaller.

Ships

This is a container ship. It carries hundreds of metal containers filled with cargo. The main part of the ship is called the hull. Inside the hull are floors called decks.

Containers

The sharp bow pushes through the water.

Tug boats

A tug is a small, powerful boat that can tow a big ship. The tug boat guides the big ship in and out of the harbor.

Turn and learn

8-9 Seas and oceans
40-41 Sport and leisure
60-61 Explorers

What is a boat with two separate hulls called?

Boats

There are many types of boat. Some carry goods or passengers, some have special jobs to do, and some are just for fun.

Fishing boats pull huge nets through the water to scoop up fish.

Lifeboats go out in stormy seas to rescue people in trouble.

Hovercraft skim across the top of the sea on a cushion of air.

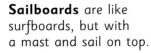
Jet skis are fun boats that skim and jump across the waves.

Sailboards are like surfboards, but with a mast and sail on top.

Sailing boats

When the wind blows, you can go sailing. The wind pushes on the boat's sails and makes the boat go forwards. This boat is a big racing yacht. The tall, triangle-shaped sail at the front is called a spinnaker.

Spinnaker

Conning tower

Most of the submarine is under the water.

S 190

Submarines

A submarine is a ship that can dive under the water. This fighting submarine (above) carries missiles for attacking enemy ships.

Fighting ships

This fighting ship is called a frigate. It has guns and missiles to defend itself against other warships and aircraft. At the back are a helicopter deck and a hangar (a building for storing aircraft).

Fumes from the engine come out of the funnel.

The radar on the mast detects other ships and aircraft.

Submersibles

Scientists use small submarines called submersibles to explore the deep sea. This submersible is called Deepstar. It can dive more than 4,000 ft (1,200 m) below the surface of the sea.

The gun turret spins around to fire in any direction.

F174

A catamaran.

Engineering

Designing and building things such as cars and towering skyscrapers is called engineering. People who do engineering are called engineers. They have to be good at science and mathematics.

The construction of the Empire State Building in New York

Engineering materials

Engineers use hard-wearing materials, such as metal, plastic, and wood. This picture from the 1930s shows a construction worker building the steel frame of a skyscraper.

Mechanical engineering

Designing and making machines, and parts of machines, is called mechanical engineering. Mechanical engineers also repair machines that have gone wrong.

Aeronautical engineers make aircraft. Here, an aircraft is being constructed in a factory.

Turn and learn

22-23 Great cities
52-53 The Romans
62-63 20th century
152-153 Space travel

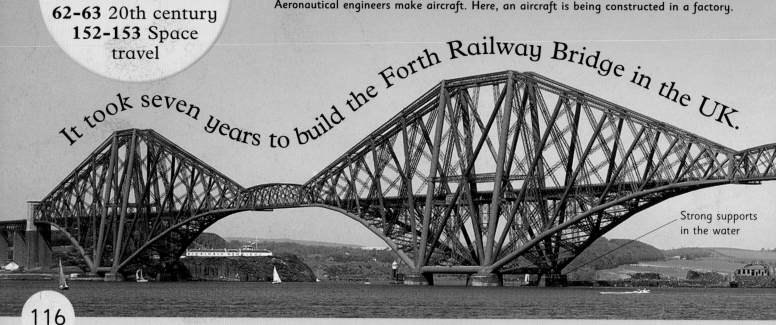

It took seven years to build the Forth Railway Bridge in the UK.

Strong supports in the water

What kind of bridge did ancient Roman engineers invent?

Engineering machines

Parts of machines are often made and fitted together by other machines. This is a car production line. As the cars move past, robots weld them together, and then paint them.

Engineering in space

Astronauts work in space to mend satellites and build space stations. Space engineering is difficult work because parts float around and the astronauts have to wear bulky space suits and thick gloves.

Robots join the car parts together with welding torches.

Designing by computer

Computer-aided design (CAD) uses computers to help design things, such as cars. The computer can show what the car will look like before the real car is made.

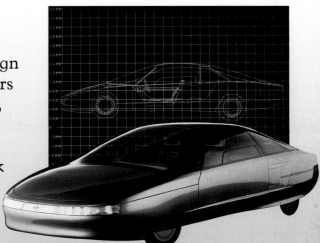

This graphic design shows the basic outline of the car.

Civil engineering

Civil engineering is designing and building roads, railroads, bridges, tunnels, dams, and tower blocks. Civil engineers work with strong materials, such as steel and concrete.

The bridge is made of huge metal tubes.

Trains cross the Forth Bridge along this track.

The arch bridge.

Machines and computers

Machines are things that help us to do jobs. Machines such as scissors are very simple. Machines such as computers are very complicated.

Operator's cab

The crane's "boom" stretches all the way across the construction site.

Simple machines

This simple machine is called a shadoof. It is a type of lever. Farmers use it to put water onto their fields. Tools such as can openers and pliers are also simple machines.

The shadoof helps this Egyptian farmer to lift a heavy bucket of water.

hands on
Rest a ruler on a pencil. Push down on one end of the ruler to lift the other end up. This is a machine called a lever. Levers help to lift weights.

This digger is digging a ditch for a large pipe to go in.

A crane is a machine that lifts and moves heavy loads.

Chunky tires

What kind of machine pulls a plow on a farm?

The first computers

The first computers were built in the 1940s. They were huge. Some, like this one, filled a whole room. But they could not do as many things as a modern pocket calculator!

This machine was called the Electronic Numerical Indicator and Calculator (ENIAC).

Computer parts

These computer parts let you control a computer and get data in and out.

Monitor is a screen where a computer shows words and pictures.

Mouse and keyboard are used for typing words into the computer.

Scanner turns pictures and photographs into data in the computer.

Printer copies words and pictures from the screen onto paper.

Computers

A computer is a machine that stores information, called data, in its memory. A computer has an electronic brain that moves data around very quickly. A tablet is a computer with no keyboard or mouse.

Laptop computer

A computer shows data on its monitor.

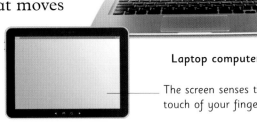

The screen senses the touch of your fingers.

Tablet computer

Construction machines

You can see lots of big machines on a construction site. They dig holes in the ground and move heavy materials around the site.

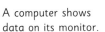
Digging arm

This robotic vacuum cleaner spins air around and around to suck dust out of carpets.

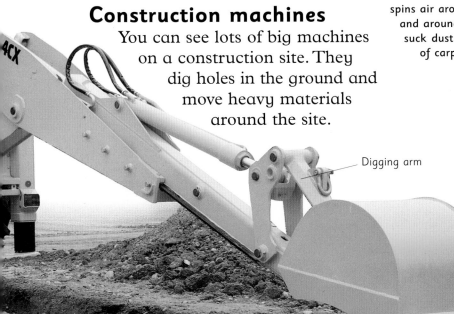

Machines at home

Vacuum cleaners, washing machines, lawn mowers, and hedge trimmers are machines that help us to do jobs at home and in the yard. They all have motors inside that move their parts.

A tractor.

Television and media

Television, radio, newspapers, magazines, and the Internet make up the media. They bring us news, information, and entertainment.

These screens show the pictures from all the cameras.

Television monitor

Television

Hosts, camera operators, sound engineers, directors, and producers are needed to make a television program. Most programs are made in rooms called studios.

A host and camera operator making a program in a television studio

The director decides what pictures and sounds we see on our televisions.

When was the first television program shown?

Radio

At the back of this picture is a radio studio. The radio hosts are speaking into microphones. The person at the front controls what the listeners hear on their radios.

Newspapers

Thousands of local, national, and international newspapers are published every day. There are also weekly and monthly magazines on hundreds of different subjects.

Writing the news

People who find news stories are called journalists. They record what people do or say and write articles that we read in newspapers, or reports for television news programs.

Daily newspapers from around the world

A multimedia website on the Internet

Advertising

You probably see hundreds of ads every day. Ads tell us about products or services that companies offer. The companies pay television, newspaper, and magazine companies to show their ads.

In towns and cities, there are ads almost everywhere you look!

Multimedia

The word "multimedia" means different media mixed together. There are many multimedia websites on the Internet. These sites show words and photographs, and also sounds and moving pictures.

121

In 1928.

Communications

The telephone, television, radio, and the Internet are different ways of communicating with people. They let us talk to each other, or send words, pictures, and sounds.

Communication satellites send messages from one part of the world to another.

Telecommunications

Television, radio, telephones, and email are called telecommunications. They send messages over long distances. The messages go through underground cables, radio antennas, and satellites.

This huge dish is an antenna. It beams messages to communication satellites and collects the messages that come back.

Simple communications

Here are some ways you could communicate without speaking.

Semaphore uses two flags held in different positions to show letters.

Morse code uses short and long beeps or flashes to show letters.

Puffs of smoke from a fire can show rescuers where someone is.

Sign language uses hand signs to help deaf people communicate.

Blowing a whistle can call for help in an emergency.

Radio

The sounds you hear on a radio travel through the air to the radio as invisible radio waves. The radio picks up the radio waves with its antenna.

An alarm clock with a radio

Which three letters mean "Help!"?

Information by light

Words, pictures, and sounds are often turned into flashes of light for their journey from one place to another. The light travels along special cables called fiber-optic cables.

The dish is aimed at the satellites in space.

Light travels along thin threads of glass inside the cables.

Telephones

A telephone turns the sound of your voice into signals that can travel as electricity, radio waves, or light. Complicated electronics connect your phone to the one you are calling.

Some mobile phones can send emails and look at websites on the Internet.

The Internet

The Internet is made up of millions of computers all over the world connected together. It lets us send emails, communicate with people in different locations, and look at websites that are stored on the computers.

You can even video chat through the Internet.

Television and video

The word "video" means moving pictures. You can watch videos on television or on a computer screen. The pictures are filmed using a video camera. Many televisions are connected to set-top boxes that can record programs, and can also display video content delivered via the Internet.

You might have a television satellite dish at home.

The letters "S-O-S."

Our planet

The Earth is the planet where we all live. It is a huge ball of very hot rock with a cool surface called the crust. Planet Earth travels in space.

Spinning Earth

The Earth slowly spins around once a day. The line it spins around is called the Earth's axis. At the ends of the axis are the Earth's poles.

North Pole

The Earth's axis goes through its poles.

The Earth's axis...

...is tilted to one side.

South Pole

The Earth's surface

There are seven huge pieces of land on the Earth's surface. They are called continents. They cover about one-third of the surface. Oceans cover the rest.

Earth as a magnet

Have you ever used a compass to find your way? It works because the Earth acts as if it has a giant bar magnet in the middle.

124

Inside the Earth

The Earth's crust is quite thin. Underneath is a deep layer of hot rock called the mantle. In the middle is a heavy core.

Core
Mantle
Crust

The cracked crust

The Earth's crust is cracked into lots of huge pieces called plates. The cracks are called fault lines. Earthquakes and volcanoes often happen where the edges of the plates grind together.

The San Andreas Fault, California

Mountains and valleys

Most mountains are made when rocks are pushed upward by movements of the Earth's crust. Blowing winds, flowing rivers, and glaciers wear away the mountains.

Sedona, Arizona

Picture detective

Look through the Planet Earth pages and see if you can identify each of the picture clues below.

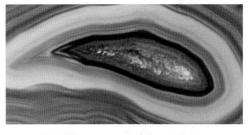

Turn and learn

4-5 World map
64-65 World of life
140-141 The universe
148-149 Earth's moon

The Pacific Ocean. It covers nearly half of the Earth's surface.

Volcanoes and earthquakes

The ground under your feet seems very solid, but in places it is weak or cracked. These places are where volcanoes and earthquakes happen.

Flowing lava
The hot, runny rock that flows out of a volcano is called lava. Lava can sometimes travel very fast, like a red-hot river.

Volcanoes are often cone-shaped mountains. The cone is made of hardened lava from the volcano.

Volcanoes
Magma is melted rock under the Earth's crust. Sometimes it bursts through an opening in the crust, called a volcano. Lots of ash and dust shoot out, too.

What is the name for a large ocean wave caused by an earthquake?

Earthquakes

When two pieces of the Earth's crust slide past each other, the ground shakes from side to side. This is called an earthquake. Earthquakes can split and crack the ground, and break up roads.

This pattern shows how the ground shook during an earthquake.

Studying earthquakes

People who study earthquakes are called seismologists. They try to figure out when earthquakes will happen, so that people have time to get to a safe place.

Reading by a seismograph (machine to record earthquakes)

Staying safe

This is the Transamerica Pyramid in San Francisco. The building has been specially designed to stay safe in an earthquake. It will shake, but it will not fall down.

Mount St. Helens erupted in a huge explosion in 1980.

Vesuvius

The Roman city of Pompeii was buried in ash when Vesuvius erupted in 79 CE. Many people who lived in Pompeii were killed.

This man covered his face to protect himself from the falling ash.

These figures are plaster casts of the bodies of people who died in Pompeii.

A tsunami ("soo-naa-mee").

Types of rock

Rocks come in different colors and patterns. The three main types of rock are named after the way they are made.

Igneous rocks are made when hot, melted rock called magma turns solid.

Metamorphic rocks have been heated up and changed deep underground.

Sedimentary rocks are made from layers of sand, mud, or sea creatures.

Rocks and fossils

Rocks make up the solid outer skin of the Earth—the crust. Rocks are normally hidden underground, but you can see them in mountains and at the seaside.

The Giant's Causeway

These strange rocks in Ireland are called the Giant's Causeway. They are made of an igneous rock called basalt. The rock cracked apart to form these shapes as it cooled down.

The Giant's Causeway is made up of thousands of columns of basalt rock.

Sandstone

Sandstone is a sedimentary rock. It is made when layers of sand get squashed tightly together, over time, on the seabed. Uluru (also called Ayers Rock) in Australia is a gigantic lump of sandstone.

The wind and rain are slowly wearing away the rock.

There are many caves around the bottom of Uluru.

What is the name for a person who studies rocks?

Minerals

Rocks are made up of substances called minerals. Different rocks are made up of different mixtures of minerals.

This mineral is called agate. It always has stripes of color.

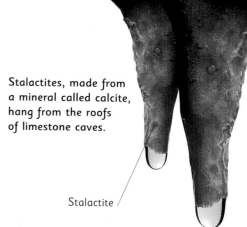

Stalactites, made from a mineral called calcite, hang from the roofs of limestone caves.

Stalactite

Ammonite fossil

Spider in amber

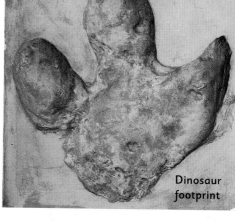

Dinosaur footprint

Fossils

Fossils are the bodies of plants and animals that lived millions of years ago. When they died, their bodies were buried and slowly turned to rock.

Trilobite fossil

Footprints in rock

Footprints left in the ground by animals millions of years ago often became fossils, too.

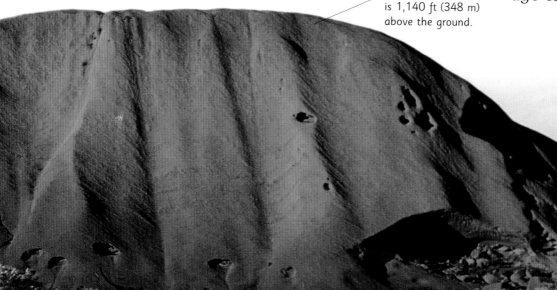

The top of Uluru is 1,140 ft (348 m) above the ground.

Turn and learn

18-19 Mountains
86-87 Dinosaurs
134-135 Water

A geologist.

Earth's materials

The Earth's rocks and minerals contain many useful materials, such as metals and gems. We also get fuels such as coal and oil from the Earth.

Hot, liquid aluminum being poured into a mold

This digger is scooping up iron ore at a mine in Brazil.

Metals

Iron, aluminum, and copper are metals. Most metals are hard, shiny materials. They come from minerals called ores. The ores are dug out of quarries or mines.

Iron ore

Getting metals out

Often, to get metals from ore, the ore must be heated until it is very hot. This is called smelting. Sometimes electricity is used to remove the ore.

130

Gems

Some minerals found in rocks look like beautiful pieces of colored glass. They are called gems. Sapphire, ruby, and diamond are all gems.

A diamond in the rock where it was found

A fully cut diamond

Cutting diamonds is a very skilled job.

Using metals

Metals are materials used for making things. Here are four common metals and their uses.

Iron has been used to make tools and weapons for thousands of years.

Copper is a brown metal. Electricity cables and coins are made of copper.

Aluminum is a lightweight metal. It is rolled thin to make foil.

Gold always stays very shiny, so we make jewelry and ornaments from it.

A ruby laser beam

Using gems

Gems for jewelry are carefully cut and polished to make them sparkle. Other gems are useful in industry. Rubies make laser light, and tough diamonds are used in drills.

A cut ruby

Coal mining

Coal is made from ancient plants that lived millions of years ago. It is a fuel for power plants and houses. Coal is found in thick layers underground.

Coal miners work deep underground, digging out coal.

Turn and learn

56-57 Aztecs, Incas, and Mayas
98-99 Energy
116-117 Engineering

Diamond.

Air and atmosphere

You cannot see, touch, or smell air, but it is all around you. There is a thick layer of air all over the Earth. It is called the Earth's atmosphere.

Why we need air

Without the air, plants and animals could not live on Earth. Air contains gases that animals need to breathe and plants use to make food.

Rising air

When air gets warmer, it spreads out and takes up more space. This makes the warmed air lighter, so it rises.

A hot-air balloon floats upward because it is full of warm air.

Gas burners in the basket heat up the air inside the balloon.

Plants use carbon dioxide from the air to make food.

How many layers does the atmosphere have?

Gases in the air

Air is made up of several different gases mixed together. We use some of these gases for special jobs.

Oxygen makes up about a fifth of the air. Nothing can burn without oxygen.

Nitrogen makes up three-quarters of the air. It is used to make fertilizers.

Helium is used to fill up balloons, which float because helium gas is lighter than air.

Carbon dioxide is used to make the bubbles in fizzy drinks.

Neon is used inside lighting tubes. The gas glows when electricity flows through it.

Earth's atmosphere

The atmosphere makes the Earth safe to live on. It keeps out harmful rays from the Sun and space. It also keeps the Earth warm.

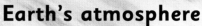

This hazy blue layer is the Earth's atmosphere, which stops rays from space hitting Earth.

Thinning out

As you go upward through the atmosphere, the air becomes thinner and colder—and it gets more and more difficult to breathe. Eventually, the air runs out. Then you are in space!

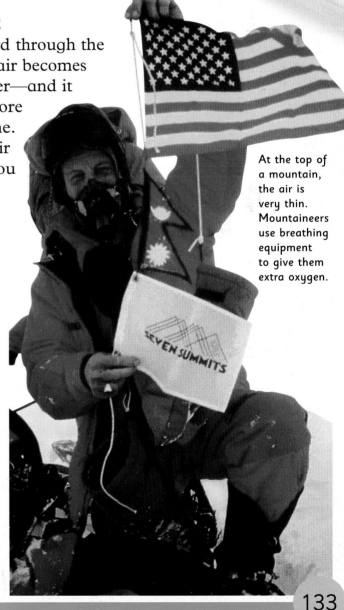

At the top of a mountain, the air is very thin. Mountaineers use breathing equipment to give them extra oxygen.

Air pollution

Cars, buses, heating boilers, and factories all put poisonous gases and smoke into the air. The gases and smoke are called air pollution.

Some gases from factories cause acid rain, which can kill trees.

Four. They are called troposphere, stratosphere, mesosphere, and thermosphere.

Water

Water is all around us. It is in rivers and seas, in the ground, and in the air. We use water from rivers and underground for drinking and washing. It comes to our homes along pipes.

Seas and oceans

The Earth's seas and oceans are full of water. The oceans cover about two-thirds of our planet's surface. That is a lot of water!

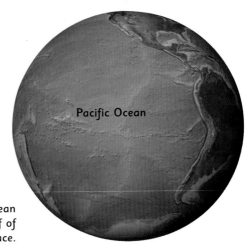

Pacific Ocean

The Pacific Ocean covers nearly half of the Earth's surface.

Water is a liquid. It always flows downward.

Water always sticks together. Small bits of water form drops.

Ice

When water gets very cold, it freezes and turns into ice. Ice is a solid. When ice warms up, it melts and turns back into water. Ice is lighter than water, so lumps of ice float.

Steam

When water gets very hot, it turns into a gas called water vapor. When this cools down, it turns back into water. The vapor from a hot kettle cools quickly when it leaves the spout, making a cloud of tiny water drops called steam.

When a hump of water moves across the surface, it is called a wave.

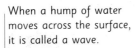

Saltwater

Have you ever tasted sea water? It is very salty. People can get salt from the sea by letting sea water dry up. Water from rain or from rivers is not salty. It is called freshwater.

134

The water cycle

Water travels between the oceans, the air, the land, and rivers.

 Water from the **oceans** and the ground goes into the air.

 When damp air rises and cools, the water turns into **clouds**.

 Water falls to the ground from the clouds as **rain, hail**, or **snow**.

 The rain soaks into the ground. Some rain water runs into **streams**.

 Water from streams is carried back to the ocean in **rivers**.

Water and the landscape

This deep canyon was made by water flowing down the Colorado River in the US. The water gradually wore away the rocks and carried the pieces away.

hands on

There is invisible water vapor in your breath. You can see it by breathing slowly on a cold mirror. The vapor cools and turns into steam.

Water for life

Plants, animals, and people need water to live. Animals have to drink water. Plants suck up water from the ground through their roots.

Elephants visit a water hole every day to drink.

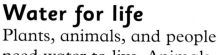

Two-thirds of your body is water.

Weather

What is the weather like today? Is it sunny or cloudy, dry or rainy, baking hot or freezing cold? The weather affects what people do and wear every day. This is why we need to know about it.

Why weather happens

The weather happens as the Sun heats the air. As the air heats up, it moves around the Earth's atmosphere. The weather helps to spread the heat and cold evenly around the Earth.

Air moves around the Earth, making wind and rain. From space, it is possible to see the clouds in the Earth's atmosphere swirling around.

Blowing winds

Wind is air that is moving from place to place. Hurricanes bring very strong winds that blow down trees and rip the roofs off houses.

Weather words

Here are some of the main features of weather. How many of them describe the weather today?

 Sunshine gives us heat and light. It warms the air and dries the land.

 Clouds are made from tiny water droplets. Dark clouds mean rain is on the way.

 Temperature measures how hot or cold the air is, in degrees Celsius or Fahrenheit. 29°

 Wind is air moving around. Winds can be light, like a breeze, or strong, like a gale. 7

 Rain is drops of water that fall from clouds. Rainfall is very good for plant life.

 Snow is made from tiny bits of ice. It falls instead of rain when it is very cold.

What is the name for a scientist who studies the weather?

Clouds and rain

Clouds are made up of tiny drops of water or tiny pieces (crystals) of ice. They are made when damp air rises upward and cools. A cloudy day often means that rain or bad weather is coming.

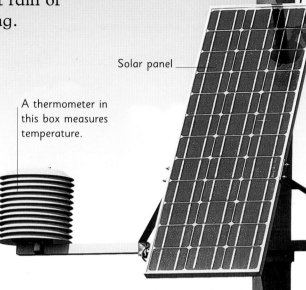

An anemometer measures wind speed.

A wind vane shows the wind direction.

Solar panel

A thermometer in this box measures temperature.

Measuring weather

There are weather stations all over the world. Special instruments measure the temperature, rainfall, wind speed, and the number of hours of sunshine.

Weather satellite

Thunder and lightning

A thunderstorm looks very dramatic. Lightning happens when electricity made inside a cloud jumps down to the ground. This makes the air heat up, which causes a loud, rumbling noise called thunder.

Forecasting the weather

Weather forecasters look at information from weather stations and pictures from weather satellites. Computers help the forecasters to work out what the weather is going to be like.

Turn and learn

10-11 Deserts
14-15 Rain forests
100-101 Electricity
70-71 Plants and food

A meteorologist.

Climate and seasons

Climate is the type of weather a place usually has over a whole year. If the place where you live has warm summers and cool winters, it has a temperate climate.

Palm trees grow in tropical climates.

Places near the equator have hot, tropical climates

Climate zones

Different places on Earth have different climates, depending on the type of weather they get during the year.

Tropical regions have hot weather all year round, with rain almost every day.

Subtropical zones are also hot all year round, but have dry and rainy seasons.

Desert climates are always dry. Deserts have hot days and freezing cold nights.

Temperate areas have warm summers and cool winters and sometimes snow.

Mountain climates are cold, and often windy, with lots of rain and snow.

Polar regions are very cold all the time—with ice, snow, and blizzards.

Extra-cold climates

The Arctic and Antarctic regions have very cold, polar climates. It is so cold that the sea freezes in winter!

How do desert ground squirrels stay cool?

Seasons

In many places, the year is made up of four seasons. They are winter, spring, summer, and fall. Each season has different weather.

Winter

Winter is the coldest season, with frost and snow. The days are shorter and it gets dark earlier in the evening.

Spring

In spring, the weather begins to get warmer. Trees and other plants grow leaves and flowers.

Summer

Summer is the warmest season. The days are very long, with many hours of sunshine.

Fall

In fall, leaves fall from the trees. Some animals hibernate, ready for winter.

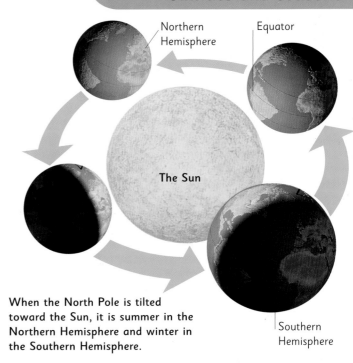

Northern Hemisphere

Equator

The Sun

Southern Hemisphere

When the North Pole is tilted toward the Sun, it is summer in the Northern Hemisphere and winter in the Southern Hemisphere.

Why seasons happen

The Earth is tilted over to one side as it orbits (circles around) the Sun. As the year goes by, different places get different amounts of heat from the Sun.

Coping with climates

Animals and plants have special features that help them to live in very hot or cold climates.

Monsoon homes

Some subtropical places have a season of heavy rain called a monsoon. Sometimes, people build their houses on stilts to keep dry.

Polar bears have thick fur coats.

They use their tails as sunshades.

139

The universe

The universe contains the Sun, the Earth, other planets, everything in our galaxy, and billions of other galaxies. It also contains all the empty space in between.

A telescope from the 17th century

The first astronomers

Astronomers have studied space for thousands of years. The Italian astronomer Galileo was one of the first to publish his findings about the things he saw in the night sky through a telescope.

Ideas about the universe

People used to think that the Earth was at the center of the universe. Galileo showed that they were wrong.

We now know that the Sun is at the center of the solar system.

The Earth travels around (orbits) the Sun.

The Sun

What is a black hole?

Life in space

In space, astronauts and their equipment float around because gravity does not hold them down like it does on the Earth. Astronauts have to learn how to live and work in space.

Handles and straps fixed in the floor keep the astronauts still, and help them to get around.

The Big Bang

Astronomers think that the universe was made about 13.8 billion years ago in an enormous explosion called the Big Bang.

Modern astronomical telescope

Picture detective

Look through the Space and the universe pages to identify each of the picture clues below.

Turn and learn

24–25 World of people
64–65 World of life
124–125 Our planet

A place where gravity is so strong that even light cannot get out.

Stars and galaxies

Our night sky is full of distant objects. The tiny specks of light we can see are stars, like the Sun. A galaxy is a huge group of stars.

Stars

A star is a huge ball of gas that gives out light and heat. Some stars are smaller than our Sun. Some are thousands of times bigger.

New stars

Far away in space there are monster-sized clouds of gas and dust. If the gas and dust clump together into a ball, a new star forms and begins to shine.

A cloud of gas and dust in space is called a nebula.

Here are the glowing remains of an old star that is dying.

Old stars

Stars shine for thousands of millions of years. But they do not shine forever. When massive stars die, they explode. The explosion is called a supernova.

What is the only galaxy we can see without a telescope?

Constellations

Thousands of years ago, people saw that the stars made shapes and patterns. They gave the patterns names. We call these star patterns constellations.

The Orion

Spotting a constellation is like doing a "join-the-dots" puzzle.

The Southern Cross

The Milky Way

All the stars you can see in the night sky are part of a huge star cloud called the Milky Way. This is our galaxy. It contains billions of stars.

Galaxy shapes

There are billions of galaxies in the universe. Some are spiral-shaped. Some are ball-shaped. Some are not really any shape at all. The Milky Way is a type of "spiral" galaxy called a barred spiral.

A spiral galaxy has long "arms" of stars.

The Andromeda Galaxy.

The Sun and solar system

The Earth is part of a family of eight planets that move around the Sun. Together, the Sun and the planets are called the solar system. The Asteroid Belt separates the inner planets from the outer planets.

Planets in orbit
The planets travel around the Sun in huge, oval-shaped paths called orbits. The orbit that the Earth follows measures almost 186 million miles (300 million km) across.

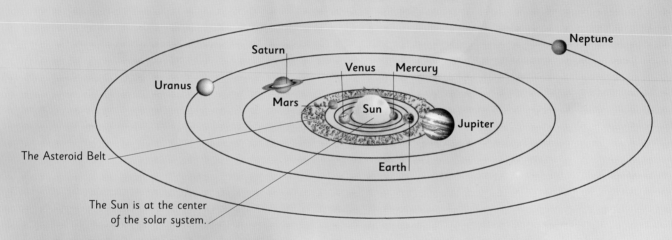

Neptune

Saturn

Uranus

Venus Mercury

Mars

Sun

Jupiter

The Asteroid Belt

Earth

The Sun is at the center of the solar system.

Orbits and spins
Planets orbit the Sun at different speeds. As they orbit, they also spin around at different speeds.

Mercury is closest to the Sun. It takes just 88 days to make its orbit.

Jupiter is the biggest planet, but it spins around in less than 10 hours.

Neptune is furthest from the Sun. It takes 165 years to make its orbit.

Our nearest star
The Sun is our local star. It is 93 million miles (150 million km) from the Earth. It has been shining for billions of years. All the heat and light needed for life on Earth comes from the Sun.

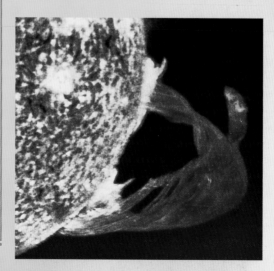

On the Sun
It is an amazing 10,800°F (6,000°C) on the surface of the Sun. Huge jets of glowing gas, called solar flares, leap up into space. Dark patches of cooler gas, called sunspots, move across the surface.

Which is the hottest planet in the solar system?

Mercury

Venus

Earth

Mars

Gas and dust
The Sun and all the planets in the solar system were made 4.5 billion years ago from a huge cloud of gas and dust.

Astronomers have discovered planets around other stars.

Planet Earth
Earth is a very special planet. It has a rocky surface, water, and an atmosphere. It is the only planet in the solar system where animals and plants can live.

Jupiter

The Sun is 100 times wider than the Earth.

From Neptune, the Sun looks like a tiny speck of light.

Saturn

Jupiter spins so fast that its middle bulges outward.

Uranus

Neptune

Cold planets
Uranus and Neptune are billions of miles away from the Sun. Hardly any heat reaches them, so they are extremely cold worlds.

145

Venus is the hottest planet. Its thick atmosphere traps heat from the Sun.

Planets and moons

The Earth is a massive ball of rock moving around the Sun. It is called a planet. A moon is a ball of rock that moves around a planet.

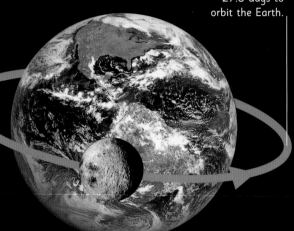

The Moon takes 27.3 days to orbit the Earth.

Earth's moon
Is the Moon out tonight? The Moon is the name we give to the Earth's only moon. You can see the Moon because light from the Sun bounces off it. Its journey around planet Earth is called an orbit.

Mars is nicknamed the Red Planet.

Mars has enormous valleys and volcanoes.

Rocky planets
The planets near the Sun are rocky planets. They have a thick crust of solid rock, and hot, runny rock inside. Mercury, Venus, Earth, and Mars are all rocky planets.

Life on other planets
This is the surface of Mars. Plants and animals cannot live on Mars because there is no air and it is freezing cold. But there might have been life on Mars millions of years ago.

The surface is rocky and dusty.

What is the biggest storm on Jupiter called?

Saturn

Saturn's rings are 20 times wider than the Earth.

Planets with rings

Some planets have rings around them. Saturn has spectacular rings. They are made up of millions of chunks of rock and ice that orbit Saturn.

Moons

There are more than 170 moons in our solar system. The force of gravity keeps them traveling around their planets. This is Saturn's largest moon, called Titan. It is larger than Earth's moon.

Titan

Jupiter's moons

Jupiter has 67 moons. Most of them are a lot smaller than Earth's moon, except these four.

 Ganymede is the largest moon in the whole solar system.

 Callisto looks like our moon. It is completely covered in craters.

 Io is red and yellow. It is covered in volcanoes that never stop erupting.

 Europa is covered in ice. Underneath the ice there is a huge ocean of water.

Gas planets

Jupiter, Saturn, Uranus, and Neptune are known as the Gas Giants. These four planets, which are extremely far away from the Sun, are giant balls of gas and liquid. They do not have a solid surface like the rocky planets.

There are enormous, swirling storms on Jupiter.

The Great Red Spot.

Earth's moon

The Moon is the Earth's traveling partner in space. It is a freezing cold, dusty place, where there is no air or water.

Only astronauts have seen this side of the Moon—the far side.

The Moon's orbit

The Moon is 239,000 miles (384,000 km) away from Earth. It moves around the Earth on a journey called an orbit. Each orbit takes 27.3 days.

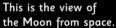
This is the view of the Moon from space.

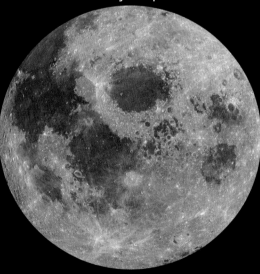

The Moon does not have weather like the Earth does.

Changing face

The Moon seems to change as it travels around Earth.

New Moon is when the Sun lights up the far side of the Moon.

Crescent Moon can be seen when a tiny bit of the near side is lit up.

First quarter Moon is when the right half of the near side is lit.

Gibbous Moon is when nearly all of the near side is lit up.

Full Moon is seen when the Sun shines on the whole of the Moon's near side.

The near side

As the Moon moves around the Earth, it spins slowly. Because it turns exactly once every orbit, the same side always faces the Earth. We call this side the near side of the Moon.

Who was the first person to set foot on the Moon?

Visiting the Moon

So far, the Moon is the only place in the solar system that astronauts have been to. In 1969, a mission to the Moon, called Apollo 11, put two US astronauts—Neil Armstrong and Buzz Aldrin—on the lunar surface for the first time.

This is the Apollo 11 command and service module. It stayed in space, above the Moon, with one astronaut, Michael Collins, inside.

Eclipses

Sometimes, the Moon gets in the way of the Sun's light. This is called an eclipse. The Moon's shadow falls on the part of the Earth that is facing the Sun and the Moon.

This is John Young and the Apollo 16 lunar module on the Moon in 1972.

Craters and seas

The Moon's surface is covered in bowl-shaped holes called craters. They were made when lumps of rock called meteorites smashed into the surface.

The American astronaut Neil Armstrong.

Comets and space rocks

In addition to the planets and moons, there are objects made of rock, dust, and ice orbiting (following a path) around the Sun. Sometimes, we see them when they come close to Earth.

Comets
A comet is a huge lump of dust and ice hurtling through space. It is like a massive, dirty snowball. There are millions of comets in orbit around the Sun. Most of them are too far away to see.

Long tails
When a comet comes near the Sun, its ice begins to melt. This releases gas and dust into space. Rays from the Sun push the gas and dust into two long tails—a dust tail (white or yellow) and a gas tail (blue).

Comet Hale-Bopp

Asteroids look a little like enormous potatoes!

A comet's tail can be millions of miles long.

Which comet flies by Earth once every 76 years?

Meteors

Have you seen a shooting star (a meteor)? A shooting star is created when a piece of dust from a comet hurtles into the Earth's atmosphere and burns up in a flash.

Big and small

Asteroids come in all kinds of sizes. Some are as small as grains of sand. The biggest one found is 572 miles (920 km) across. It is called Ceres.

Only the very biggest asteroids can be seen from the Earth.

The Asteroid Belt

An asteroid is a lump of rock going around the Sun, like a tiny planet. There are billions of asteroids between Mars and Jupiter. This area is called the Asteroid Belt.

Meteorites

Sometimes large lumps of rock collide with planets and moons. These are called meteorites. They crash into the surface—leaving huge, bowl-shaped holes called craters.

Mercury

hands on

Put some flour in a saucer and smooth it flat. Dip your finger in water and let a drop fall into the flour. Did you make a good crater?

Mercury's thin atmosphere does not provide much protection from meteorites.

Many of Mercury's craters are hundreds of miles wide.

Space travel

Astronauts are people who travel into space. They do science experiments, fix the space station, and find out what living in space is like. One day, they might even travel to other planets.

The payload (cargo) that the rocket is carrying

Launch tower

Rockets

Astronauts cannot get to space without a rocket. At the bottom of the rocket are very powerful motors. They send out jets of hot gas that push the rocket upward into space.

The first rockets

This is Robert Goddard, an American rocket maker. In 1926, he built the first rocket that used liquid fuel. Today, most rockets that travel into space still use liquid fuel.

The rocket engines start and then... lift off!

Mission Control

Mission Control is a command center on Earth. Here, engineers and scientists direct space missions. They decide when rockets take off and make sure everything is working correctly.

Fuel tank

Motors

52

Space station

Astronauts live and work in a huge spacecraft called the International Space Station (ISS), which orbits around the Earth. The ISS is the largest artificial body in space right now. It is likely to be in operation until 2024.

Solar panels

International Space Station (ISS)

Walks in space

Astronauts sometimes walk outside their spacecraft to do repairs. They wear special suits that contain an air supply. The suits also protect them from harmful rays in space.

Astronaut controls spacesuit by adjusting switches.

There is no air in space.

The space shuttle *Atlantis* landed like an airplane but needed a parachute to help it to slow down.

Turn and learn

The space shuttle

Rockets can only be used once—but the space shuttle flew back to Earth at the end of each mission and could be used again and again. The last space shuttle was used in 2011.

153

The *Salyut 1*, launched by the Soviet Union on April 19, 1971.

Space exploration

Astronomers and astronauts have learned lots of amazing things about the universe. But there are still many things to discover.

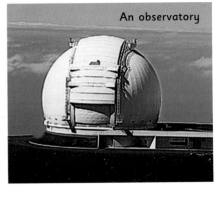
An observatory

Telescopes

Inside this dome is a large telescope. It has a huge mirror that collects light coming from space. Telescopes make planets and stars look much bigger, helping us to see these distant objects more clearly.

A radio telescope has a huge dish that can collect lots of radio waves at once. It also collects rays coming from space.

Radio telescopes

Some objects in space, such as black holes, cannot be seen with ordinary telescopes. Astronomers search for them using radio telescopes that can detect the radio waves given out by materials about to fall into these holes.

What was the first spacecraft to land on a speeding comet?

Space telescopes

Telescopes on Earth sometimes get a blurred view of space because the Earth's atmosphere gets in the way. Telescopes orbiting the Earth, such as the Hubble Space Telescope, give a much clearer view.

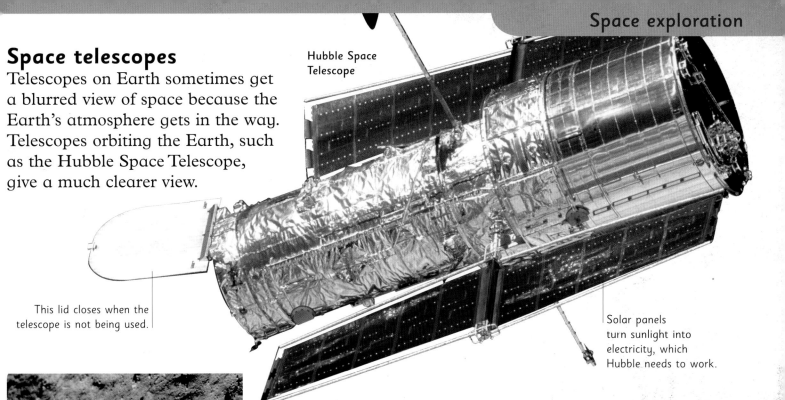

Hubble Space Telescope

This lid closes when the telescope is not being used.

Solar panels turn sunlight into electricity, which Hubble needs to work.

Man on the Moon

When astronauts visited the Moon, they did experiments and collected rocks. Their footprints, left in the dusty surface, will last for millions of years.

Missions to Mars

One day, astronauts might visit Mars. It will take six months to get there, and six months to get back. Unmanned space probes have already been to Mars.

Robot vehicles like the *Curiosity* are exploring the land on Mars.

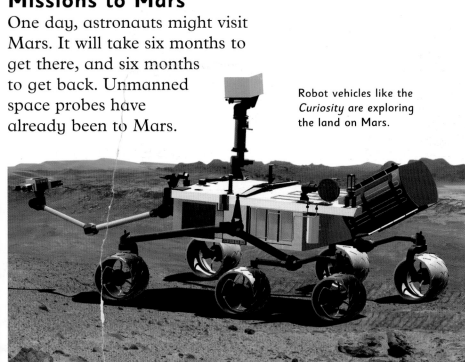

Space probes

Robot spacecraft are called space probes. They take photographs and use instruments to find out about planets and moons.

 Luna 3 took the first photographs of the far side of the Moon in 1959.

 Pioneer 10 was the first space probe to fly close to the planet Jupiter.

 Voyager 1 flew past Saturn, taking photographs of its rings and moons.

 Pathfinder landed on Mars with a robot vehicle that explored the surface.

 Huygens is studying Saturn's moons, mainly Titan and Enceladus.

 Spirit rover landed on Mars to find out if there had ever been water on the planet.

The *Philae*, which landed on the Churyumov-Gerasimenko comet in 2014.

True or false?

Can you figure out which of these facts are true and which ones are made up?

1 Everyone has different fingerprints.

2 A tree's length can be calculated from the rings on its trunk.

3 In addition to digging, a digger picks up heavy loads.

4. True 5. False—it is called the Red Planet 6. True 7. True 8. True

4 Knights were soldiers who fought on horseback.

5 Mars is called the Crimson Planet.

7 Ganesha is a Hindu god.

6 Punch and Judy are puppets from Britain.

8 Kangaroos carry their babies in pouches on their bellies.

Answers: 1. True 2. False—a tree's age can be calculated in this way 3. False—it only digs holes.

Quiz

Test your knowledge
with these quiz questions.

4 Which game is played with a puck and flat sticks?

A: Basketball   B: Football
C: Table tennis   D: Hockey

5 Where did gladiators fight?

A: The pyramids   B: The Forum
C: The Red Fort   D: The Colosseum

1 Where does the cactus store water?

A: Stem   B: Thorn
C: Leaf   D: Roots

2 How many legs does an insect have?

A: 8   B: 6
C: 4   D: 20

6 Where is the San Andreas Fault?

A: Cairo   B: Sydney
C: California   D: London

7 Where did the Maya people live?

A: Central America   B: Mexico
C: Egypt   D: Rome

3 What kind of gas is used to fill hot-air balloons?

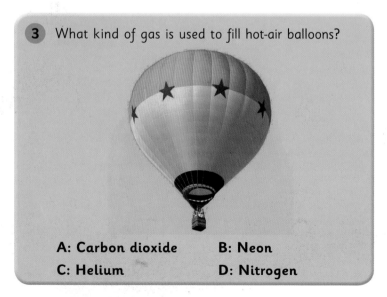

A: Carbon dioxide   B: Neon
C: Helium   D: Nitrogen

8 Who is the Greek goddess of love and beauty?

A: Zeus   B: Athena

C: Aphrodite   D: Hades

9 How many teeth does a crocodile usually have?

A: 80   B: 50

C: 100   D: 70

10 Which of these is a fungi?

A: Mushroom   B: Cactus

C: Palm tree   D: Fir tree

11 Where do emperor penguins live?

A: Arctic   B: North Pole

C: Antarctica   D: Scandinavia

12 How many bones are there in your skeleton?

A: less than 50   B: more than 300

C: less than 100   D: more than 200

13 How many years ago was the Jurassic period?

A: 208–146 million   B: 250-208 million

C: 146–65 million   D: 65–30 million

14 What is the deep layer of hot rock inside the Earth called?

A: Mantle   B: Core

C: Crust   D: Pole

15 Where do Jewish people meet for worship and prayer?

A: In temples   B: In synagogues

C: In mosques   D: At home

16 Which planet is closest to the Sun?

A: Mercury   B: Mars

C: Venus   D: Jupiter

Answers: 1:A 2:B 3:C 4:D 5:D 6:C 7:A 8:C 9:A 10:A 11:C 12:D 13:A 14:A 15:B 16:A

Who or what am I?

Can you figure out who or what is being talked about from the clue?

Stagmatoptera

2: I am an insect and I use my legs to row across water.

Viking

Cat flea

Water boatman

Sikh warrior

1: I was a soldier and had to buy my own weapons and armor.

Leaf

Roman soldier

Hoplite

Lockheed Martin

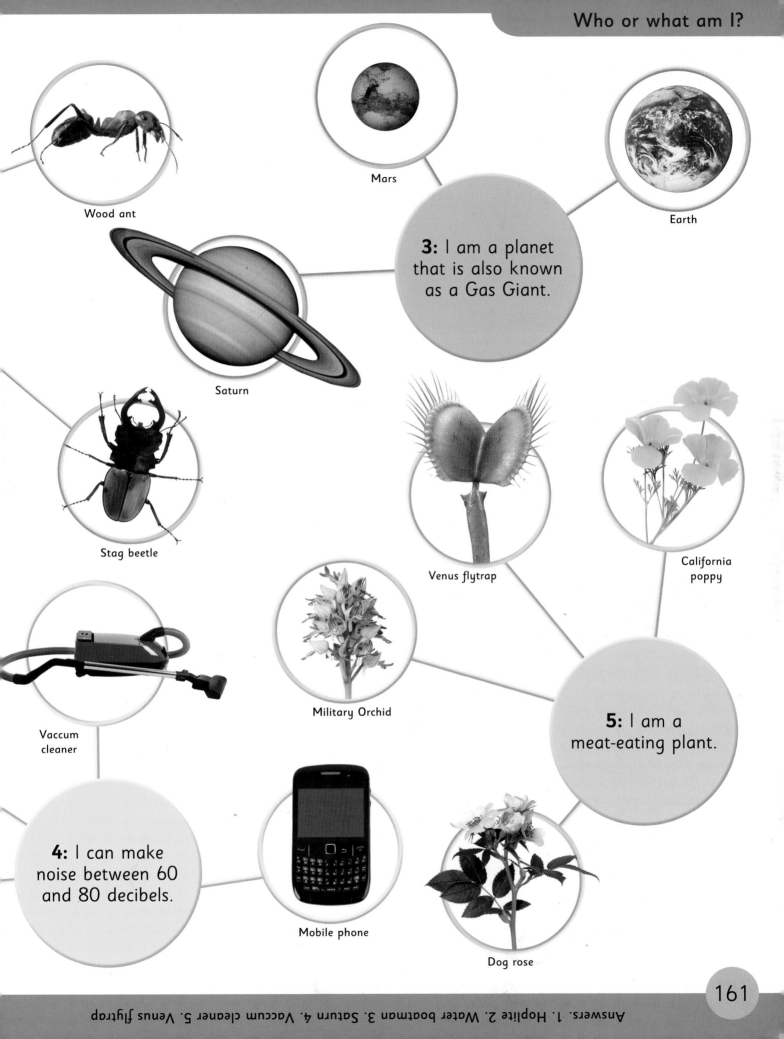

Wood ant

Mars

Earth

3: I am a planet that is also known as a Gas Giant.

Saturn

Stag beetle

Venus flytrap

California poppy

Vaccum cleaner

Military Orchid

5: I am a meat-eating plant.

4: I can make noise between 60 and 80 decibels.

Mobile phone

Dog rose

161

1: This building in the US has been designed to not fall down in an earthquake.

2: This Arctic animal can travel using huge pieces of ice as rafts.

3: This bridge in the UK is made of huge metal tubes.

10: These rocks in Ireland are made of an igneous rock called basalt.

12: This temple is in the Mayan city of Tikal.

11: This ancient South American city was built by the Incas.

Where in the world?

Match the description of each animal or landmark with the pictures and discover in what part of the world they can be found.

Forth Bridge

Sydney Opera House

Eiffel Tower

Polar bear

Machu Picchu

Spiny anteater

Opera House 8. Mountain gorilla 9. The Sphinx 10. Giant's Causeway 11. Machu Picchu 12. Temple of the Great Jaguar

4: This is the most famous landmark of Paris, the French capital.

5: This monument in India was built by an emperor for his wife.

9: This stone statue guards the pyramids at Giza in Egypt.

6: This Australian mammal lays eggs in a tiny pouch on its belly.

8: This widely hunted African animal is now very rare.

7: This building in Australia has a winglike roof, made to look like the sails of boats.

Taj Mahal

Temple of the Great Jaguar

Mountain gorilla

Giant's Causeway

Transamerica Pyramid

The Sphinx

Answers: 1. Transamerica Pyramid 2. Polar bear 3. Forth Bridge 4. Eiffel Tower 5: Taj Mahal 6. Spiny anteater 7. Sydney

Glossary

ammonite Extinct group of marine animals

ancestor Person who lived a long time ago to whom you are related by birth

architecture Art and science of designing and constructing buildings or other structures

armor Protective covering, often made of metal, worn by a warrior

axis Center line around which the Earth rotates

blizzard Extremely heavy snowstorm with strong winds

burrowing Digging a hole in, through, or under, the ground

camouflage Colors or patterns that help an animal to blend in with its surroundings

civilization Culture and way of life of people living together in an organized and developed society

continent Huge piece of land usually divided into different countries. Africa is a continent

crust Hard, outer layer of the Earth

decibel Unit used to measure the loudness of sound

desert Very dry area of land with little or no plant life

digestion System by which food is broken down and absorbed in the body of a living thing

DNA Substance present in most living things that carries instructions for making cells

domesticate To train or breed animals to be useful to humans

empire Group of countries or states governed by one ruler

fingerprint Mark made by the tip of your finger.

fossil Remains, or impression, of an ancient animal preserved in rock

glacier Mass of ice that moves slowly under its own weight

gladiator Trained fighter in ancient Rome who battled other fighters or wild animals in a public arena

government System by which a country is ruled; the group of people who make the policies and laws for a country

gravity Force that pulls objects toward each other. It keeps the Earth in orbit around the Sun, and your feet on the ground

harvesting Act of gathering ripe crops from a field

Internet A "network" of connections that enables computers anywhere in the world to exchange information

Inuits Group of peoples who live in the Arctic regions of North America and Greenland

invention Any thing or process that has been created and is completely new and unique

jet engine Engine that mixes air with fuel, burns it, and pumps it out to push an aircraft forward

legend Story handed down from the past and believed to be true

mineral Solid, natural chemical substance that is found in rocks

nuclear power Energy released when the centers of atoms break up, during a "nuclear reaction"

orbit Path traveled by a natural or an artificial object around another object in space

orchestra Large group of musicians who play together on a variety of instruments. They are led by a person called a conductor

physics Science and study of matter and energy

pyramid Ancient structure made from stone or brick. It has a rectangular base and four triangular sides meeting in a point at the top

reflex Automatic movement of your body that you can't control

rover Vehicle designed to explore the surface of a planet or moon

satellite Object that rotates around a planet in space. The Moon is a satellite of the Earth

scavenger Animal that feeds on the remains of dead animals

seismograph Machine that measures earthquakes

shrine Place where people go to worship a god, holy person, or event

skyscraper Very tall building with many levels

spacecraft Vehicle that can travel in space

tribe Group of people with a shared culture, language, and customs. They often share blood ties

tropical Describes regions near the equator that have hot climates

waterhole Natural pond or pool that is used by animals as a drinking place

Index

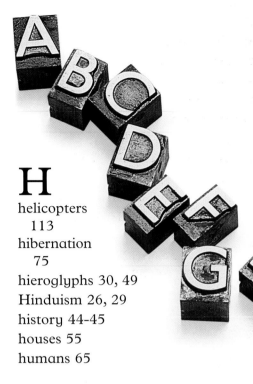

Key to measurements

Length, distance, and area
km = kilometers m = meters
cm = centimeters ft = feet in = inches
square km = square kilometers
Speed km/h = kilometers per hour
mph = miles per hour

Weight and volume kg = kilograms
g = grams lb = pounds
Temperature °C = degrees Celsius
°F = degrees Fahrenheit
Years and dates years BCE (Before Common
Era) = the years before the birth of Jesus Christ

years CE (Common Era—"in the year
of the Lord") = the years since the birth of
Jesus Christ
Very large numbers
1 million (1,000,000) = 1,000 x 1,000
1 billion (1,000,000,000) = 1,000 x 1 million

Acknowledgments

Dorling Kindersley would like to thank:

Andrew O'Brien for original graphic artworks; Chris Bernstein for compiling the index; Lisa Magloff, Amanda Rayner, and Penny York for editorial assistance and proofreading; Jacqueline Gooden, Claire Penny, Mary Sandberg, and Cheryl Telfer for design assistance; David Roberts for DK cartography; Angela Anderson and Sean Hunter for additional agency picture research; Sally Hamilton, Rose Horridge, Sarah Mills, and Charlotte Oster for DK Picture Library research; Charlie Gordon-Harris for in-house assistance; David Holland for the use of his traditional "Punch and Judy" puppets; and Victoria Waddington for photo shoot assistance.

Picture credits

Dorling Kindersley would like to thank the following for their kind permission to reproduce their photographs / images:
(Key: a = above; b = below; c = center; l = left; r = right; t = top)

Aerofilms Ltd.: 53br. **AKG London:** 57tl. **Apple Computer, Inc.:** 119c. **Ardea London Ltd.:** John Mason 10-11. **Associated Press AP:** 121br; John Rasmussen 54. **Dick Bass:** 133br. **Board of Trustees of the Armouries:** 59tcr; 59tr. **Booth Museum of Natural History:** 75bcl. **British Airways:** 113br (*Concorde*). **British museum:** 24cb, 45bl, 47cra, 48bcl, l, 49ca, cra, 51cra (book), 53tl, 57tr, cr. **Britstock-ifa:** 134bl. **Brookes and Vernons/JCB:** 118-119b. **By permission of the British library:** 30tc, tr. **Cairo Museum:** 44tr. **Bruce Coleman Collection:** 17br, 69ca; Atlantide 52cr; Jane Burton 85ca; Jules Cowan 11tl; M P L Fogden 76cbl; Christer Fredriksson 17tr; Sir Jeremy Grayson 64l; Johnny Johnson 20-21; Hans Reinhard 27tl; Slidefile 16l ; Pacific Stock 60cla. **Corbis:** 60-61; Roger Antrobus 51tc; Archivo Iconografico, SA 46cal; Bettmann 63tc, 119tl; Lloyd Cluff 125c; Ecoscene 62-63c; Macduff Everton 21tr; Eye Ubiquitous 50cr; Ales Fevzer 1cl, 40l; Gallo Images 19c; Lindsay Hebberd 37cl; Chris Hellier 12cl; Angelo Hornak 116-117; Charles and Josette Lenars 53b, 87cr; Steve Mayer 115cr; Buddy Mays 13cl; David Paterson 18-19; W. Perry Conway 79r. Photo B. D. V. 39tl; Paul A. Souders 117cli; David and Peter Turnley 63bc; Brian A. Vikander 18c; Ralph White 61crb; Adam Woolfitt 98l; Michael S. Yamashita 37t. **Corbis Stock Market:** 122tl; Firefly Productions 120bl; Lester Lefkowitz 114; Kunio Owaki 135tr. **Denoyer-Geppert Intl.:** 93br. © **Disney Enterprises, Inc.:** 41bc. **Dorling Kindersley:** The Science Museum, London 63crb, Jerry Young 162bc, 162br. **Philip Dowell:** 75cb (zebra). **Dreamstime.com:** Benis Arapovic 25tc, Kitchner Bain / Kitch 123crb, Buriy 35cra, Orcea David 30bc, 119c, Jose Manuel Gelpi Diaz 95c, Sonya Etchison 158bc, Eric Isselee 160crc, Andrej Kaprinay 121crb, Ldprod 123cl, Richard Moody 32cla, Mphoto2 122bc, Vladimir Ovchinnikov 119cb, Punchman 157c, Scanrail 63tc, 123tc, Sooyewguan 109bl. **Alistair Duncan:** 26bcl, 27cr, 42l, 47tl, 48cr, 49tl, 52l. **Dyson-Staubsauger:** 119br. **EasyInternetCafé Ltd., 2002:** 123cr. **ECM Records:** 35cra. **Ecoscene:** Andrew D. R. Brown 127br; Tweedie 130l. **Educational and Scientific Products Ltd.:** 92b. **E & E Picture Library:** R. Nathwani 29tr. **Empics Ltd.:** Tony Marshall 40tr. **Environmental Images:** Martin Bond 99br. **E. S. A.:** 155crb. **Mary Evans Picture Library:** 61tr. **Financial Times:** 31cl, 31r. **Ford:** 118cr. **Gables:** 27br, 62c, 75cb (yak), 100c. **Genesis Space photo library:** ESA/CNES/Arianespace 2000 152r. **Getty Images:** George Doyle/Stockbyte 157tr, Frank Krahmer/Photographer's Choice RF 159clb. **Glasgow Museum:** 27crb, 29c. **Tory Gordon-Harris:** 56l, 134-135. **Hasbro:** 41tr. **Robert Harding Picture Library:** 39c, 108l, 109bl;

Mohamed Amin 27tr; Jeremy Bright 26l; Tettoni Casio 28cr; V. Englebert 56cr; Alain Evrard 24l; Warren Faidley/Int'l Stock 136bl. Robert Francis 57c; Fred Freiberg 17clb; Srulik Haramaty 131c; Simon Harris 68c; Miwako Ikeda/Int'l Stock 32-33; Ronn Maratea / Int'l Stock 82t; Lousie Murray 14l, 139bl; R. Rainford 32c, 53c; Sunstar/Int'l Stock 112tl; Valder Tormey/Int'l Stock 105tr; Dr A. C. Waltham 18cl; S. Westcott 10tl. **Simon Holland:** 37b. **Hulton Archive:** 116tl, 152cl. **Hutchison Library:** Robert Francis 58cla; Melanie Friend 23c; Nick Haslam 6br; Tim Motion 16br; Chris Parker 118cl; Bernard Regent 11br; Leslie Woodhead 124-125cb. **The Image Bank / Getty Images:** Ezio Geneletti 134cb; Jeff Hunter 75cal; Izan Petterie 22tcl. **INAH:** 56br. **Jewish Museum, London:** 29tl. **JPL:** 147bl (Callisto), 147bl (Europa), 147bl (Io). **Dr Marcus Junkelmann:** 52bl. **Lebrecht Collection:** Odile Noel 34l. **Dinesh Khanna:** 33c. **Barnabas Kindersley:** 20bl, 28bc, 38bc, br, bcr, 39bl, bc, br, bcr. **Mattel UK Ltd.:** 41cb. **Chris Mattison Nature Photographics:** 78-79t. **Reproduced by Permission of the Henry Moore Foundation:** *Locking Piece* (1963-64) 32cr. **Mountain Camera / John Cleare:** 19br; Colin Monteath 20c. **Museen der Stadt, Wien:** 35clb. **Courtesy of the Museum of London:** 30bc, 131cl. **Museum of Mankind:** 60cl. **Museum of the Order of St. John, London:** 53clb. **N.A.S.A.:** 45c, 117tc, 136-137, 144bc, 146bl, br, 147tc, c, br, 148tr, cr, bc, 149tl, 151br, 155tr, cl. **NASA/GRIN:** 63c, 106c, 137cr, 142c, 142br, l, 145all, 148-149a, 148l, 149cl, 153tr, 153c, 153br, 155bl, 155br. **NASA:** JPL/Space Science Institute 147cl, 155br, 161tr, ESA 155crb, JPL 144bl, 161cla, JPL-Caltech 153tc, 155bl. **NASA/NSSDC:** 150-151. **NASA's Planetary Photojournal:** 19tr. **National Maritime Museum:** 60cr, 115b. **National Motor Museum, Beaulieu:** 110bl. **Natural History Museum, London:** 14clb, 46tl, 46cl, cla, 65bc, 83c, 83c, 87tl, 130br, 131tl. **N.H.P.A.:** B & C Alexander 9cra; A. N. T. 81b; Joe Blossom 79cl; Mark Bowler 15cr; Stephen Dalton 76bl, br; Martin Harvey 12-13, 128-129; T. Kitchin & V. Hurst 79br; Stephen Krasemann 20cr; Tom and Therisa

Stack 17c; Dave Watts 74-75; Martin Wendler 15tl. **NOAA:** 124tr. **Nokia, 2001:** 63tr, 123t. **Stephen Oliver:** 30c, 31bc, 97cl. **Oxford Scientific Films:** Ben Osborne 100l; John Brown 67tr; Warren Faidley 137bl. **Performing Arts Library:** Fritz Curzon 36cb. **Pictor International:** 8cl, 115tc, 116c, 128c. **Pitt Rivers Museum, University of Oxford:** 35cl, 46cb, 46br, 122bl (fire). **Planetary Visions:** 1cr, 124-125b. **Popperfoto:** Reuters 121tr. **Powell-Cotton Museum:** 27cl. **Ram Rahman:** 58cl. **Redferns:** Nicky J Sims 35c. **RNLI and crew, England:** 115cla. **Morten Jensen:** 33cb. **Robert Harding Picture Library:** R. Kiedrowski 28l. **Royal Botanic Gardens, Kew:** 15tr. **Royal British Columbia Museum:** 47b. **Royal Geographical Society Picture Library:** 61cr; Gregory 61tl. **Guy Ryecart:** 109rc, 155br (*Voyager*). **St. Bride Printing Library:** 31tc. **Science Museum:** 111cra, 155br (*Voyager*). **Science Photo Library:** Doug Allan 21tr; W Bacon 19tl, Sid Bahrt 82bc; John Bavosi 94br; Martin Bond 137c; Dr. Jeremy Burgess 140cl; Alan and Sandy Carey 75cb (cheetah); Ron Church 115crb; Crown Copyright/Health & Safety Laboratory 131br; Bernhard Edmaier 138bc; ESA/Photo Library International 146tr; European Southern Observatory 143br; Simon Fraser 89c; Maximilian Stock Ltd 43br, 152bl; John Mead 68bc; Peter Menzel 103tl; NASA 42cr, 133tr, 141ca, 153tc; National Cancer Institute 96l; David Nunuk 154l; David Parker 123tl, 138l; Pekka Parviainen 150c, bl; BSIP Dr. T. Pichard 91cl; Quest 90-91b; Restec, Japan 7bl; Royal Observatory, Edinburgh 140-141cb; Peter Ryan 122-123b; Dr. Robert Spicer 16tr; J Steinberg 83bl (pelican); Geoff Tompkinson 96br; US Library of Congress 97bl, 112cr; Jeremy Walker 118l, 133bl; David Weintraub 126-127; Frank Zullo 140-141t, 143tr, 149tr, 151t, Photodisc/Joshua Ets-Hokin 160bc. **Search and Rescue Hovercraft, Richmond, British Columbia:** 115cl. **Senekenberg Nature Museum:** 86br (Cretaceous), 86br (Jurassic). **Neil Setchfield:** 32cl. **Sony Computer Entertainment Europe:** 41tl. **Statens Historika Museum, Stockholm:** 55cr. **Still Pictures:** Adrian Arbib 99tl; Roland Seitre 130cr. **Stone / Getty Images:** Daryl Balfour 135br; Michael Busselle 68l; Brad Hitz 92l; Tony May 69b; Stuart McClymont 65tc; Dave Nagel 106l; Robert Yager 127tc. **Telegraph Colour Library / Getty Images:** Gary Bell 8-9, 9bc; Gary Buss 139tl, cla, cl, clb; Jim Cummins 93bl; Michael Goldman 50br; David Nardini 81r; Stan Osolinski 74l; V. C. L. 57b; VEGA 1tl, 132l. **University Museum of Archaeology and Anthropology, Cambridge:** 57cra. **Volkswagen Group:** Richard Leeney 2, 109cl. **Wallace Collection:** 59c. **Alan Watson:** 15tc (vine). **Weatherstock:** 126c, 136-137t. **Janet and Roger Westcott:** 111tr. **Westminster Cathedral:** 26cb. **Weymouth Sea Life Centre:** 80bcl, 81c. **Jerry Young:** 75bl, cb (fox), 78cl (alligator), 79ca, 84tl, bl, 139br.

All other images © Dorling Kindersley

For further information see: www.dkimages.com